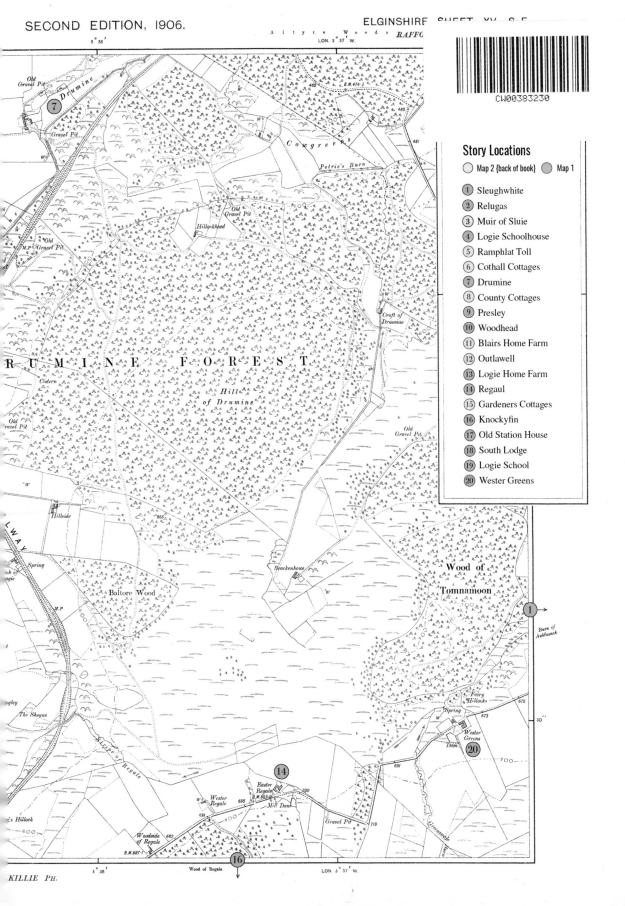

SECOND EDITION, 1906.

ELGINSHIRE SHEET XV. S.E.

CW00383230

Story Locations

○ Map 2 (back of book) ● Map 1

1. Sleughwhite
2. Relugas
3. Muir of Sluie
4. Logie Schoolhouse
5. Ramphlat Toll
6. Cothall Cottages
7. Drumine
8. County Cottages
9. Presley
10. Woodhead
11. Blairs Home Farm
12. Outlawell
13. Logie Home Farm
14. Regaul
15. Gardeners Cottages
16. Knockyfin
17. Old Station House
18. South Lodge
19. Logie School
20. Wester Greens

The Register

Dedicated to *George Macaulay Pratt*, a Logie Schoolhouse loon,
remembered by friends as a pillar of the community.

27 February 1932 – 16 November 2021

'Once upon a time..'

That's how a story might begin. For me, though, this story started twice.

I discovered the old Admission Register tucked away on a shelf in the office where I work at Logie Primary. The book was still just about in one piece, its spine held together by powdery Sellotape, its pages listing every child who had come into this school in Dunphail, a rural community in Moray, over nearly a century from 1881 to 1979. In its closely written lines, the children numbered in the order of their enrolment, I saw the possibility of 1,500 individual stories – or more, I supposed, as each one would vary depending on who was choosing to tell it.

As I turned the pages, it wasn't so much the family names that jumped out at me, although many were familiar, some with descendants among the 39 pupils now at the school: it was the farm names, the crofts, the houses and estates, home to a scattered population just south of Forres. I ran my eye down the list: Presley, Outlawell, Drumine, Cothall, places I pass every day, all within easy reach of the school. The one I stopped at, though, was Sleughwhite, the house where in my mind this story had really begun.

It's an abandoned farm which I often visit, set high on the hill above my house. I like to think that I'm not romantic about life up there, but I have no real idea of how tough it must have been. There would have been little time or inclination to stand and gaze north across the Moray Firth as I do, and if anyone did, it would more likely have been to see what the weather was bringing than to admire the view. Of all the many ruined farms and crofts I know, though, it's one I can never visit without wondering who lived there once, and although no one has ever caught me doing it, I always call out at the door when I visit, as it feels as if someone might be home. The steadings stand in ruins, rusting farm machinery lying where it was last left, but the roof is intact and the staircase can still be climbed, although only barn owls, flying in and out of the gaping windows, choose to use the bedrooms now.

The register, I realised, was offering me the chance to find out more about the child who had lived at Sleughwhite as well as those who'd been at Presley, Outlawell, Drumine and the rest. What had become of them? What memories had they left behind or might they still be holding in their heads? What had they dreamt of doing? Had they ever got the chance to do it? I put a notice in the *Forres Gazette* looking for people whose names or whose ancestors might be in the register.

I began to hear the stories of pupils from the past, one from a woman of 90 whose mother joined Logie School in the early years of the last century. Mary Pratt told me that whenever she struggles to sleep, she imagines herself walking the fields and tracks of her childhood, counting not sheep but farms and getting to fifty, unthinkable now in the era of far fewer tenants. This image of Mary exploring in her mind the paths of her younger life inspired me to ask our storytellers to do the same, thinking back to the farms, crofts and houses of their childhoods and answering a simple question: 'What do you remember?'

In the telling of their stories, presented here in order of the year the children joined Logie School, we hear how things changed over the century: in healthcare, in farming, transport and travel and teaching; in women's work at home and in employment; in the attitude to children born outside marriage and in personal ambitions. These memories of individual lives, along with original archive research to help tell two of the earliest tales, offer a glimpse into the evolution of this rural community. Thank you to every one of our storytellers for sharing their lives in these pages.

Moira Dennis,
Administrator, Logie Primary School, 2022

Lenny Nicol, Sleughwhite.

'My dad said, "That's where my folk used to be,
it was just a wee croft." And that was it.'

Sleughwhite • Lachlan Nicol

And so here I am. I had started out wanting to know more about Lachlan Nicol, the child who had lived at Sleughwhite and – thanks to the register – I'm sitting in a living room a few miles away in Forres having tea with his grandson and his wife Linda. He too is a Lachlan, known as Lenny, and I'm ready to ask all sorts of questions.

I'm forgetting that the Nicol family is like almost every other, including my own: few of us ask the right questions until it is too late.

•

Entry no. 671 in the register tells us that Lachlan Nicol joined Logie School in April 1898, just short of his twelfth birthday. Trace your finger across the columns to the right and you'll see that he had moved from Half Davoch School, one of several schools in the area at that time, eventually to close in 1960 and now a house. Living at Sleughwhite, he would have had to pass his old school on the way down the hill to his new one. I ask his grandson Lenny if he knows why that might have been, but almost nothing about the family was passed down to him from his own father. 'He pointed out Sleughwhite one day, when we were up for a run, and said, "That's where my folk used to be, it was just a wee croft." And that was it.'

In a way, of course, it doesn't matter at all. The detail of Lachlan's everyday life in Dunphail will always take second place to what happened to him later.

Just before Christmas 1916, while working as a horseman on Dunphail Mains Farm, Lachlan was conscripted and went to Elgin to enlist with the 1st Battalion Seaforth Highlanders. That trip of twenty miles was the start of a journey around the world: Lachlan served in India, Egypt and Palestine, where he was injured. Having survived for four days in hospital, Lachlan Nicol was to die just a week before the end of the war there.

And so my mind comes back to Sleughwhite. Was the news sent back to his parents or to his wife? I ask Lenny if anything of his grandmother's life has been handed down to him by his father. Again, the answer is brief: 'Nothing whatsoever.'

I know that every thread I pull will bring with it more questions, but those empty rooms at Sleughwhite still need filling with more than my imagination.

•

What I know about Lachlan Nicol's life and war service comes from research carried out by Mark Laing, who published the military record of every man on the Edinkillie War Memorial for the centenary of the Armistice in 2018. I noticed that Lachlan's wife Annie had been a widow when they had married in 1915 and I wondered what impact the loss of a second husband would have had on how she lived her life. I know that she and Lachlan had at least one child, because here I am drinking tea with the next generation, so how had Annie managed?

I turn to ScotlandsPeople, the archive of the National Records of Scotland, and find that all the references to Annie Nicol's early life can be located within a mile or two of the school. She had been born Annie Miller Duncan in Edinkillie in 1880, her mother Isabella Miller, a domestic servant living at Glassfield who married a farm servant of Carnoch, George Stephen, when Annie was fourteen months old. Annie's illegitimate status, marked on her birth certificate, was to follow her throughout her life.

We know nothing about Annie's growing-up years but the certified landmarks of life – birth, marriage and death – are easy enough to trace. She was still living at Glassfield when she married her first husband at Bogton Place in Forres. He was George Duncan, a farmer from Outlawell, who by coincidence had the same surname as his bride. Their wedding took place on 23 April 1909, when she was 28 and he was 26.

I knew that the marriage was not destined to be a long one: Annie and her second husband, Lachlan Nicol, had married just six years later. Yet when I find the record of George Duncan's death, I need to check and double-check what I am reading.

Annie and George's marriage had lasted just four days. The death certificate of 27 April 1909 tells us that George was killed by meningitis following a bout of influenza. The only detail the registrar notes about his widow is that she was 'Ann Miller, illegitimate.'

I turn to the *Forres, Elgin & Nairn Gazette* of Wednesday, 5 May 1909, to see if their story merited a mention. In what I expect to be a local paper, I find a full account of world news: the report of a five-hour speech by Lloyd George, outlining his war budget, the Boer War over but still sending shockwaves through the country's finances; news of the Queen of Holland giving birth to a daughter, seen by the nation as some sort of defence against the swallowing up of their country by the German Empire; and the deposition of the Sultan of Turkey. There are advertisements appealing for migrants from Forres to head for Canada, with pictures of Scottish immigrant farmers standing proudly in their own corn; plenty of cures for hair loss; and, for sale, a green Brazilian parrot – a good talker, apparently. There in among them is the tiny death announcement for Annie's first husband George, with no mention of their marriage just days before.

•

Six years later, in 1915, Annie is 35 and a housekeeper. In November, she marries Lachlan Nicol, the boy from the Logie School register now aged 29, in a wedding ceremony not in Edinkillie church, as I might have imagined, but in the manse. Their son, another Lachlan, named after his father and grandfather, is born seven months later, on 5 June 1916. Earlier that year, just weeks after the wedding, conscription had been introduced for all men between the ages of 18 and 41, and when the baby is six months old, his father heads for Elgin and enlists.

He didn't come home from the war, but his baby son grew up to be the father of a Lachlan of his own, the man known as Lenny who's here in his living room offering me more tea. The war story and the death overseas seem always to have been at the forefront of the family story, Lachlan's name unveiled on the Edinkillie war memorial in 1921 but his widow Annie never fully in focus.

I find her record. She died in 1930 at the age of 49 after an operation at Dr Gray's hospital in Elgin. She'd been living in Bank Lane in Forres at the time and her death, three days before her son's 14th birthday, was registered by George Stephen, the man she had grown up with as a father, no longer a farm servant but a retired railway worker. Here, even on her death certificate, under Name, Surname, Rank or Profession of Father, I see noted that George was 'afterwards' married to her mother. The word itself might not have been used, but Annie Nicol was as illegitimate at her death in 1930 as she had been at her birth in 1880.

•

The trouble with delving through records as a starting point is that individual deaths take on a disproportionate importance in any family story. They are easy to find, life stories harder to trace. The Lachlan who died in Palestine had five siblings, many of whom would have had longer and happier lives. I found a photo in the *Gazette* of George Stephen and Isabella, Annie's mother, celebrating their Golden Wedding in 1931, the year after Annie's death. Lives had gone on.

But what had happened to Annie's son, an orphan? His own son Lenny, who's telling me what he knows about his ancestry, was told nothing. 'My father didn't talk much about his life and his relationships because he couldn't.' I later, by chance, find him in a 1928 photograph of Dunphail School, just a couple of miles to the south of Logie, taken two years before his mother's death. Lenny does know that his father went on to join the Royal Navy, survived service in World War Two and came home to Forres. He married Sally and spent forty years as a postie, living to 1991. Lenny was to do the same job, for five more years than his father. The generations rolled on and the tradition of a Lachlan in every one of them continues, either as a first or middle name.

My story about Sleughwhite, then, is not the one I thought it would be. I'd set out on a search for the Lachlan Nicol whose name is in the Logie School Admission Register and on the war memorial at Edinkillie church. Instead, I'd found his widow and baby son and met that boy's own son too. I realise, though, that despite all the questions, there was one I hadn't thought to ask. Among all those Lachlans, had there ever been another Annie in the Nicol family? I call and ask Linda but, of course, I'd forgotten: no one had even known the name.

Mary Pratt, Relugas.

*'Right to the top of the brae, right down to
the bottom of the village, carrying two pails of water..'*

Relugas • Margaret May Watt

Margaret Watt, always known as Rita, would never have been short of a good pair of boots for her three-mile daily walk to school from Relugas: her father, John Watt, was the shoemaker in the village. He made and mended boots for the men who worked on the farms of the area. Those farms are still clear in the mind of his granddaughter, Mary Pratt: this is the woman who – now aged 90 and sometimes struggling to sleep – walks the old roads in her mind and counts the farms along the way, in the days when they all had tenants. As Mary points out, those tenancies and the number of men working on the local estates had a huge impact on the life of the area: 'Fifty more farmers to go to the kirk, for one, and families for the school.'

Mary's mother, Rita Watt, was born in 1903 and joined Logie School when she was eight, entered into the register as number 856. Her brothers and sister – Willie, Mary, John and George – had gone there before her, although the register tells us that the eldest two had done some schooling first at Relugas. Her memories of the walk to Logie, passed down to her daughter, were mainly of running to hide if they saw the minister up ahead – so while the kirk might well have been fuller on a Sunday, it would have been with unwilling children – and jumping into fields to take a neep if they ever got hungry on the way. That hunger for turnips would have been down to the walking, though, and not to poverty: while Rita's father was the shoemaker, her mother ran the Post Office, where Rita worked until she married Frank Grant of Glenernie and they moved to farm at Gervally at the top of Relugas. Rita, the youngest, was the only one of her siblings to stay in the area, the others all moving south although still within Scotland, her sister becoming head typist at a hotel in North Berwick.

Rita and Frank brought up three children at Gervally and it was hard. Mary, who like Rita was the youngest of her family, remembers how very cold the farmhouse was, the cooking done on a range. Rita's parents had retired to the farm, so seven members of three generations of the family were there, with a spare room somehow always kept for guests. Mary wonders now, looking back, where they had all slept. With no water to the house, Rita had to walk from the farm down to the bottom of the village and carry two pails of water back up, even – as she later told her daughter – when heavily pregnant. This changed when Sir Robert Grant of Logie Estate passed by Relugas one day. Seeing Rita doing her washing outside, he had a wash house built for her and water put in.

Frank and Rita kept Aberdeen Angus cattle, black and red, taken by a dealer; they grew oats and tatties and kept hens, so their family ate well. During the war years at Gervally, Frank would cycle the eight miles to Forres to try to sell the few tatties he'd produced but would sometimes have to cycle them the eight miles home again as well. Over the years, though, the farm business grew and the family began to sell eggs to the butcher in Forres. Mary loved working on the farm, remembering the bib and braces she'd wear and the fun when squads of ladies from Forres would come out by bus to lift the tatties.

The comings and goings of other families in the register shows how tenuous employment could be for hired hands but the farm servant at Gervally was more established. Rayburn – his first name John was never used, just as Mary's father was never anything but 'the boss' – came to the farm when Mary was six and by the time he left, when he was nearly 70, she was married to George.

Rita's daily walk to Logie School, wearing the boots her father had made, turned out to be the furthest regular trip away from Relugas that she would ever make. She remained in the village all her life and died in 1982, aged 79, a year before her husband, just as the major changes in tenancies were making themselves felt in the area. She would rarely have gone into Forres, as vans from the butcher, the grocer and the draper would bring whatever she needed to the farm; her children were grown up by the time she went beyond Moray, to visit her sister in North Berwick; and she certainly never left Scotland. Relugas was where she'd grown up; her farm and her family were there. What reason would there have been to leave?

Tina Fraser, Muir of Sluie.

*'It was such a tiny house. They must just
have slept where they found room..'*

Muir of Sluie • Chrissie Young

The Cause of Leaving column in the Admission Register, if it was used at all, was generally populated with Education Finished, Left the District or a straightforward move to another school.

Chrissie Young joined Logie School in 1916 at the age of six and was entered into the register as number 916. She caught my eye as the first to have her cause of leaving entered – bluntly – as Dead, with a bold full stop but no date given.

Wanting to know the story, I searched online at ScotlandsPeople, the archives of the National Records of Scotland. One document gave me a clue to the next. In the space of a few hours I had traced the line of Chrissie's life and that of her family but the story I had uncovered was so grim that for a month or so I put off writing it up. I wanted, if not a happy ending – although I did later find those words written in my notebook, a bit of wishful thinking – then at least to know that some offshoot of Chrissie's family had thrived. And an hour ago, I got a call from Forres that told me yes, it had, so I can begin to tell her tale.

•

Stories drawn from this register are like big pictures seen through a crack in a door. It is easy to focus on a particular sorrow or joy and forget that to either side, in other branches of the same family, those joys or sorrows might be known but not keenly felt, stories heard but not lived. Within each house in this project there will have been moments of every kind of emotion, but what happens to one branch of a family quickly becomes just an episode in a much longer tale. What happened to this family, though, tells us something broader about their lives and the community around them.

Chrissie Young's time at Logie School was very brief. She arrived on 20 April 1916 but just over a month later, on 29 May, she died of diphtheria in Leanchoil hospital in Forres. Leanchoil had been opened in 1892, financed by the philanthropist Lord Strathcona – or Donald Alexander Smith as he had been, before leaving Forres for Canada to make his fortune. Getting to hospital would have offered Chrissie a chance of survival, but I wondered how a sick child from a poor family would have covered the seven miles from Sluie. There were cars in the district: the register tells us that Clementine and Betty Grierson, just a few lines above Chrissie, were the daughters of the Logie Estate chauffeur. Did Leanchoil have its own transport? Would the doctor have helped? However she made the journey, though, it was made too late. Chrissie died after being ill for eight days, her death registered by a Dr John Adam, who also crops up in the records of what is now the Town Hall, caring for war-wounded soldiers there.

I began to imagine the feeling at Logie School when word came through that the new girl from Sluie had died of diphtheria. The crowded schoolroom would be steamy, damp clothes drying in the warmth of the fires at either end. Diphtheria spreads in droplets. Children were most likely to contract it and for many the infection would prove fatal. Maybe that stark word 'Dead' in the register was written quickly, in fear.

•

Looking more closely at that death certificate of Chrissie's, I noticed another layer to the story. By the time the six-year-old died, she had already lost her mother, and the little girl's death was registered by an aunt, Jessie Fraser.

I hunted for clues to what had happened. It turned out that Chrissie's mother, Kate Young, had contracted measles and pneumonia and died just over a year before her daughter, in 1915. She had been 40. It was noted that she was a widow and, looking further, I found that her death had come just six months after that of her husband John, Chrissie's father, at the age of 41. He had been a ploughman and cattleman and his death certificate offers an insight into the treatment a working man could expect. 'Cause of death: general debility. Duration of disease: five years. Medical attendant by whom supervised: no regular medical attendant.'

John Young had suffered general debility since his mid-thirties: did he simply have too hard a life?

The family had lived on the Black Isle in Easter Ross, and turning back to the Logie register, I saw that four more Young children besides Chrissie were entered on the school register: the eldest, Jessie, was 11 years old when her little sister died. Jessie had joined Logie School less than a month after her mother's death in 1915, along with her sister Katie and brother Andrew. Chrissie had joined the school a year later and died after those first few weeks, while Maggie came in a year after that. This, then, is a family of orphan migrants living forty or so miles from home, taken by their mother's sister Jessie and her husband James Fraser, a shepherd, into their tiny two-roomed but-and-ben at Muir of Sluie.

Taking another look through the Logie register, I see that Jessie and James Fraser had three sons and a daughter of their own go through the school: Willie, James, John and a daughter, also a Chrissie, only the two youngest the same sort of age as the newcomers. Just when the Frasers at Muir of Sluie might have expected a very hard life to ease a little, then, with fewer mouths to feed, less water to carry from the well at Sluie to the house and more room in their tiny home, it would have done quite the opposite.

And that's when I stopped looking for what had happened next, half-fearing to find out more, hoping that Jessie, Katie and Andrew Young had longer and happier lives than their sister Chrissie but knowing how much would have depended on good luck. I was also struggling to know where to look, especially with names that crop up so frequently.

Until a neighbour says, 'But didn't Tina Fraser in Forres have family at Sluie?' I get in touch and yes, in two small steps through time, I have a direct line back from 2021 to 1916. Tina tells me that her father was James, one of the two older children brought up in Muir of Sluie before the arrival of their orphaned cousins. From Tina (who is, of course, Christina and could just as well have called herself Chrissie) back to her father James Fraser, and from James to his orphaned cousins, I am forging a link with the Black Isle children in the Logie register.

I can ask Tina if she knows what happened to Chrissie Young's brother and sisters, but I'm nearly scared to.

●

Tina Fraser meets me with a laptop in her hand and it's a shock to realise that I might see pictures of the people I've been thinking so much about. They have seemed too distant to have been captured on film. Here's Jessie, though, the eldest of the Young family, probably aged about 70, short and slight, wearing an apron and smiling into the camera outside her house in Brodie.

Tina tells me that Jessie had married an Angus Gillies and moved to 'a beautiful wee cottage, like Muir of Sluie.' A perfect home for two, though, rather than the unimaginably crowded conditions which Jessie must have endured growing up. They kept a lovely garden and lived a happy and very quiet life, Angus venturing by bike into Forres to stock up with paraffin at Pat Mackenzie's, where Tina worked behind the counter, but never going far afield. Tina knows about other Youngs, too: Chrissie's sister Katie married and moved away to England, while her brother Andrew went to Canada and joined the army. Tina tells me, too, about the Fraser children, her uncles and aunt: Willie, who survived the war but bore the pain of shrapnel wounds for the rest of his life; John, a shepherd; and Chrissie, a cook who had worked at Sanquhar and died in her kitchen, so the family story goes, taking cakes from her oven.

●

In Edinkillie churchyard I find the grave of James Fraser and Jessie Young, the couple who gave a home to their orphaned nephew and nieces from the Black Isle. But of Chrissie Young, who died after just a few weeks at Logie School, I can find no trace and no burial record in the Moray archives: it's possible that her body was placed in the Tombie, a small stone enclosure on Altyre Estate that is said to have been reserved for people who died of communicable diseases. It now matters more that the name Chrissie Young was entered into the Admission Register in 1916: the child's brief life at the school did not go unmarked and we are prompted, still, to tell her story.

No: 1233, Randall Pratt, Logie Schoolhouse.

'It broke my father and mother's heart, the way we went..'

Logie Schoolhouse • James Barrie Pratt

The first entry in the register by James Barrie Pratt, the headmaster of Logie School for more than thirty years, is 1105, Mary Helen Tough, who joined on 16 April 1929. Talking to his sons George Macaulay Pratt and James Randall Pratt, always known by his middle name, I'm reminded, though, that the register is always just a way into a story and never the story itself: they tell me that their father first came to teach there a year earlier, in 1928. George, Randall and their late brother Angus were to become his pupils and it seems he was harder on them than on any other children. 'What he said, went,' says George. It must have been tricky for all of them to combine their school and home lives, for his father once told Randall that he'd have sent them to Dunphail School instead, had he had the choice.

Unlike his wife Annie Macaulay Main, who had trained at college in Edinburgh, James had not set out to teach. He had sailed to Canada as a young man to join his brother in farm work, the men who were seeking employment disembarking at various stages along the St Lawrence to stand in line and wait to be hired by local farmers. James later moved on to work at the Mint in Ottawa and was with the Hudson Bay Company when war broke out in 1914. Wanting to join a Scottish regiment rather than a Canadian one, he returned home and enlisted with the Gordon Highlanders, fighting in France but incurring such a serious wound to his arm that he was never returned to the Front.

That injury stayed with him all his life, his left hand always clenched. I wonder if the war had affected him emotionally, too, but his sons both laugh at the very idea.

I ask if the other children at Logie School liked him. 'Well, I didn't like him, for a start!' George, who joined as pupil 1210 in 1937, still remembers the burning in his hand – hotter than the stove chimney in the classroom – from the belting he got with the Lochgelly tawse, a narrow, heavy strap which was used as part of the daily routine in most Scottish schools of that era. He'd been throwing snowballs in the playground.

Randall demonstrates how the strap would be administered, up the hand and onto the wrist, rather than across the palm, as I'd always imagined. And misdemeanours could be smaller: anyone failing to hold their slate pencil properly would get a rap on the knuckle from Mr Pratt, wielding his ruler as he passed their desk, just to remind them. Yet when I suggest to Randall that his father might not have been popular in the area, he looks really shocked, and I realise I'm confusing liking and respect. Their father was a man who would stand up for his politics, speak out at public meetings, face down MPs and be happy to challenge authority in an era when children were expected to salute the landowner's car as it passed.

James had become a teacher after leaving the army and completing a degree in agriculture, starting at Lhanbryde for the sum of £30 per month. He took the senior class at Logie School while his wife taught the younger children in the classroom next door, and while it's easy to characterise James as strict and Annie as gentle, Randall is keen to point out his father's generosity. His sons saw how his role as headmaster extended well beyond the classroom. In school, he looked out for the children's wellbeing in the days before the National Health Service, supplying concentrated orange juice, cod liver oil and dried milk, George and his brothers choosing to help themselves only to the first. In the wider community, he was one of the driving forces behind plans for a community hall in Edinkillie, built in the late 1920s by Jim Mackay and a team of local farmers.

James wanted a university education and success for his family. In his mind, says Randall, his sons were lined up to be a doctor, a dentist and a minister. On the other side of the family, Annie's father, a fisherman, wanted them to join him on the boats at Burghead, just along the coast. The boys, though, had ideas of their own.

When he was 16, George came home one Friday from Forres Academy and announced to his parents that he was never going back. On the Sunday, he woke to the news from his father that he would be getting on his bike and cycling the three miles to a job at Glenferness garage. Without a say in it, he had been given a future with cars, although when he'd been at school there had only been four of them in the area: one at Presley, another at Blackloch, a third at Logie House and the Pratt family's own. After a six-year apprenticeship and work at Macrae and Dick in Inverness, George became the owner of Dunphail Garage, while Randall, too, was set up in a job by his father, at Altyre, once James had realised that he didn't want to go to university.

'I was the weed amongst my brothers, but all three of us ploughed our own furrow,' says George, Randall and Angus both going on to make lifelong careers from gardens, Randall beginning at Altyre, growing vegetables for Gordonstoun school which had a base there at the time, moving on to Dunecht near Aberdeen and to the Royal Botanic Gardens in Edinburgh, ultimately becoming the curator of a flourishing botanic garden near Cardiff. Angus, too, did well in horticulture and became the Director of Parks in East Kilbride. In the garden at Logie Schoolhouse, though, their father infuriated them by continuing to plant in perfectly straight lines, as he always had, while informal planting was what they were learning far from home.

Was their father ever proud of them? He certainly never showed it but Randall, he's sure, has read somewhere – he just can't remember where – that their father was pleased by their successes. It just wasn't the thing to praise children to their faces, so none of them ever really knew.

Robert Hope, Ramphlat Toll.

'It's amazing what can be found from a visit to the loft..'

Ramphlat Toll • Margaret Lawrence

Peggie Lawrence stored away two copies of the *Forres, Elgin & Nairn Gazette* of 22 July 1953 and kept them all her life. I'm looking at one of them now, nearly seventy years on. The front page features several wedding photographs. In the bottom left-hand corner is Peggie's own: 'Married in the Old Parish Church, Nairn, on Wednesday, Miss Margaret Lawrence to Mr Thomas Hope, Bonnyrigg, Midlothian ...' And, above it, in the top left-hand corner, is that of 'Sir William Gordon Cumming, Bart., of Altyre ... to Miss Elisabeth Hinde, eldest daughter of Major-General W.R.N. Hinde, O.B.E., D.S.O., A.D.C, and Mrs Hinde, Green Place, Stockbridge, Hampshire.'

Major-General Hinde was unmatchable that day in terms of letters after his name, and he had as his new son-in-law the laird of Altyre, but it was only the Lawrence/Hope wedding that got a full write-up of its own. For Peggie wasn't the only bride outside the church in Nairn: next to her in the newspaper photo is her sister Elizabeth, always known as Betty, who in a double wedding had married Mr Robert Taylor, also of Bonnyrigg. Both Lawrence brides wore white taffeta and carried red roses; both couples went on a motoring honeymoon in Scotland. The *Gazette* even tells us that, for going away, Peggie chose a lilac and lemon checked two-piece suit with white accessories, while her sister chose a pale blue coat, accessorised with navy.

The conjunction of the Lawrence and the Gordon Cumming weddings delighted Peggie, and it delights her son Robert Hope, who has sent me the newspaper and is telling me her story.

The two sisters who married their husbands at the same time had also met them at the same time. They had gone to help out on a Darnaway Youth Club camping trip to Mellon Udrigle near Ullapool where two former RAF men from Bonnyrigg, who'd both served in India during the war, happened to be stopping over on a motoring tour of Scotland. Two years later, after the double wedding and the honeymoon, Peggie moved to the Falkirk area and then to Bonnyrigg, following her husband's teaching career. Every summer and sometimes at Easter, though, she would bring her family back to the Forres area to see her parents, pointing out as they drove past the house where she'd been born: Ramphlat Toll.

It's a place now marked only by the two very tall and distinctive yew trees on the western side of the Grantown Road, two miles or so from Logie Primary as you head to Forres. Robert later sends me a photo of Peggie's maternal grandmother standing at the door, one of the yew trees to her right, and by that point grown to only twice her height or so. The house, demolished in probably the early 1960s, was where generations of the family's children had been born, but it wasn't what you'd call Peggie's childhood home, as no single place was. Her father Robert was a farm labourer and moved from house to house, maybe depending on where he was needed, maybe as his family grew. By the time Peggie was at Logie School, in 1935, the family were living at Blair's Farm Cottages on Altyre Estate, before moving at some point to a cottage by Dounduff Farm and, as far as Robert knows, from there to Whitemire on Darnaway Estate.

Peggie, then, entered in the register as number 1190, was the only child of the family to attend Logie School. Her younger sister Betty, brother Robbie and, last of all, Jessie went to Relugas School, and it's likely that Peggie went there too at some stage. She is marked in the register as having Left the District, though, and in other entries that implies much further afield than Dounduff or Whitemire. Did the family go away for a while? The major frustration of these pages is that the Exact Date of Leaving column was only rarely completed, so it's hard to know.

Whenever Peggie did leave Logie and wherever she went, she did take something long-lasting with her: her friendship with the girl whose name is right above hers in the register. Peggie Lawrence and Jeannie Falconer were born just a fortnight apart and Robert tells me that they knew each other all their lives, a visit to Jeannie in New

Elgin joining a look at Ramphlat Toll as a regular point of interest on family holidays. Both women's sons joined the police force, Peggie's son Robert the class instructor to Jeannie's son, so the link went through to the next generation, the families celebrating together at Ian's passing out parade.

A third holiday stop-off, less obviously appealing to Robert as a child, had been the cemetery in Pluscarden. He'd sit in the car, squashed between his older brother James and their younger sister Lorna while Peggie and her mother wandered past the graves of the Ogilvies and Winks, her mother's side of the family, her great grandparents lying in pride of place to the left of the gate. As a child, Robert never really saw the point. I think of him now, though, sifting through photos from the loft, unfolding those newspapers. That's just a version of those visits by his mother to the graveyard, I suppose: something to see, to touch, keeping people long gone in the forefront of our minds.

No: 1234, Margaret McKenzie and
No: 1472, Barbara Souter, Cothall Cottages.

'You thought you knew the difference
between our planes and the German ones...'

Cothall Cottages • Margaret Dick (McKenzie)

Margaret Dick was looking forward to a hero's welcome from the headmaster. It was a terrible winter, and the snowdrifts by the road were so high that the bus – which even in fine weather could never stop halfway up the brae at Altyre for fear of not starting again – had not made it through from Forres to Cothall. So a group of six children, including Margaret, had decided to walk the three miles to school instead. They knew their mothers would never have let them – although there wasn't much traffic on the road, even on a good day – and they would never have wanted to do it if they'd been told they had to, but they knew that the teachers at Logie School would be pleased to see them.

But Margaret remembers to this day a surprising and sudden change of mood as they arrived. 'Mr and Mrs Pratt got the shock of their lives. We were soaking wet, of course. The snow plough had been through so we were bundled into Mr Pratt's little green Austin 7, all six of us, and taken home for a right row. Not a bit of 'Thank you so much for coming!''

There's a similarly sudden about-turn in mood towards the end of my conversation with Margaret and her sister Barbara, who went to Logie School in 1952. We've been discussing their brother Gordon and his successful career in the railways, when talk turns to the younger of their two brothers. Alan was training to be a stonemason but was killed on 24 May 1958, along with Allan Robertson, the son of the Altyre gamekeeper, also in the Logie register, when both came off their motorbikes by the Mundole turning. It's what I think of, even today, as the bad bend as I drive from the school into Forres. Their brother was just eighteen years old. Or eighteen and a half, as Margaret tells me: young enough, I see, for every month of his life to be counted. She shows me a photo taken just before the accident: 'He was a handsome lad.'

When we talk about memories, we can mean something recalled, often acknowledged to be half-remembered, embellished in the telling or embroidered for effect. They can, though, be as clearly defined and enduring as the writing on the Logie register page. Here we are, sitting round Margaret's table, and the weight of grief from more than sixty years ago is palpable as we run our fingers down the list of names.

●

The war was probably underway by the time Margaret and her friends decided to strike out on their own through the snow, but the only real difference it made to children at Logie School was that they had another thing to forget as they got off the bus: their gas masks. Thinking about things like blackouts and rationing was for their parents to do at home. The fact that the airfield at Kinloss was a target did mean that bombers would pass overhead, although Margaret thought she could tell the German ones and would know if they were coming to invade. The war came close once, a bomb landing near home on Altyre Estate, to the left of the road that leads to Rafford. Among the trees opposite Blair's Loch there is still a crater, and Margaret's father William took her to see it when it was freshly made. Working as the forestry foreman on the estate, he was needed at home and did not have to go to war.

No one in those days came to Logie School from Forres: it was filled with the children of farmers, estate workers and farm servants. With vans calling by at home, from the butcher, the draper, a couple of bakers and the grocer, a trip to Forres was not an everyday event. The bus would go on a Saturday, and if the children needed a haircut, say, they would have the choice of taking the bus either there or back and walking the rest, the trip always being made just after payday at the end of the month. Their mother would give them the money for a pie and they'd call by an aunt of theirs who lived in Forres, for a cup of tea and some pennies to spend, after ages choosing, in the sweetie shop in North Road.

Margaret's school memories – of pencils screeching on slates, of graduating to jotters only in year four or five; of boys pelting girls with snowballs as they went to the outside toilets; of two classrooms, the larger one with a fire burning at one end and a stove at the other, for warming hands and drying gloves – are still very vivid. She recalls the vocabulary: the banky (a word still in use today) for the slope running away from the back of the school, and beddies for hopscotch, but the skipping rhymes and songs they'd sing as they threw a ball against a wall? They're gone unless someone can sing them to remind her.

The school was unquestionably a country school, more homely than the town schools, with plenty of time with the teachers for each child. No one wore uniform and there were no school lunches, the children getting Ovaltine and Horlicks from Mr Pratt to keep out the cold – 'He was very, very good to us' – and bringing a sandwich and a play piece with them from home. With the only fruit in wartime being apples, brambles and rasps from the gardens nearby, the family was lucky one week to get two oranges. The girl next door, an only child, made hers last for hours, piercing it with a knitting needle, sucking out the juice, relishing the fruit that no one else had a claim to, while Margaret had to share hers half and half with Gordon. 'For years and years, I wished for the day when I could have a whole orange all to myself.'

Margaret did well in life, managing a draper's shop in the High Street and later running a wool shop of her own. Before that, she'd spent five years as a telephonist in Inverness yet never managed to fulfil an early dream: to work as a telephonist on a cruise ship. As we speak, I have a sudden vivid image of Margaret, alone in her cabin, far out in the ocean, eating an orange all to herself and having to share it with no one.

•

By the time Margaret's sister Barbara went to Logie, starting fifteen years after Margaret had joined, things had changed a little but not as much as I might have expected. Logie was still distinctly a country school, and the family chose to continue as before, sending their youngest child the three miles south rather than the three miles north to the town.

Some things had moved on: the days of making knickers in sewing class had passed and the boys no longer learned to knit (not that Gordon ever had, he'd always got Margaret to do his rows) but they still helped Mr Pratt in the school garden. At home, things for the Dick family were easier as the older children had left school. Logie had started to provide lunches, cooked in the school kitchen and, as always, it's the puddings which evoke the happiest memories: for Barbara, it's the thought of chocolate crunchie with warm custard that takes her straight back.

It was a big enough step for children from a small school like Logie to progress to Forres Academy, but by the time Barbara moved up, her brother Alan had been killed and the family had moved from Cothall. Sir William Gordon Cumming had come to call after Alan's death to offer the family a house on his newly acquired Sanquhar Estate in return for fire-watching duties, so the focus of the family shifted from Altyre. Barbara went on to work as a hairdresser with Fernari before marrying and having a family of her own, William continued to work at Altyre, but the family only rarely again went south along the road past Logie School, where Margaret had walked as a child so confidently through the snow.

No: 1300, Pat Morrison, Drumine.

'I remember them all being slaughtered.
And then we got a tractor, and it wasn't the same.'

Drumine • Patricia Falconer (Morrison)

The age of mechanisation came suddenly and shockingly to Drumine. The farm had seven heavy horses, Patty having as her favourite a large chestnut mare with a white nose. She recalls the size of the great hooves as the horse lay on the grass, the small girl at its feet. And then all seven were struck by grass fever, slaughtered on the farm, loaded up and driven away from Drumine on the back of a lorry. Overnight, a new era had begun. Did anyone talk to her about it? 'You just accepted it'.

Acceptance becomes a theme in our conversation. Patty accepted the fact that her plans to become a nurse, as her sisters did, were destroyed by illness. And acceptance must have got her through that illness, too, when the doctor ordered her to go to bed and stay there for a year. She was 17.

Up till then, Patty would get the half past five bus from Dunphail on a Saturday to go to the pictures in Cumming Street, staying on for chips and sometimes the second bus home. For a while she'd been feeling tired, and her mother had been applying poultices to black lumps which had appeared on her arms and legs: Pat shows me the scars she still has. One Saturday evening she decided to leave the film early and (in the days of weekend consultations) visited the doctor. He sent her straight home and although he'd promised to call by the next week, appeared at the farm on the Sunday morning, catching her breaking the rules by sweeping the floor when she should have been in bed. She had TB, he said. Her father had told her to stay away from the cows but she'd always loved to spend time with the calves, just as she had with the horses.

A new bed was installed by the window in the parlour, so that Patty could see the comings and goings of the house, only heading upstairs every night to sleep. She was allowed out of bed to wash but otherwise passed her days doing painting by numbers, reading and sleeping, knowing that if she broke the rules, she'd be spending twelve months in hospital instead.

Plenty of friends came by to see her, including her closest, Sandra Piercy, two below her in the register. And so did the doctor, every day, even two of them sometimes, most likely, she says, because they liked a run to Drumine with a cup of coffee on offer and fresh eggs and vegetables to take away. Or maybe she was sicker than she knew. Pat's granny Mary, who was deaf and blind and lived at Drumine with the family, had lost her sight at 17: I imagine echoes of that time running through the house. A lung X-ray every month and doses of what still felt like a new drug, streptomycin, meant that Pat recovered, but after a year in bed she could barely walk to the gate. She accepted the advice of the consultant that nursing would be too exhausting a career for her and instead moved to lodge with a cousin in Inverness and became a telephonist, a job that required her to sit down all day. The war had changed life for women in some professions, if not all: no one expected her to give up work when, at 21, she married Colin Wilson, the son of the blacksmith in Caroline Street in Forres, and she worked till 50, retiring to look after her mother.

Patty Falconer, then, after that year spent at home, took with her a very clear picture of the rooms in which she grew up. Drumine was a nice house, she says, with a bathroom (she thought everybody had one), the parlour and a sitting room, but 'It was cold!' and that word is said with real feeling. She was the youngest of four: along with her brother James and sisters Isabelle, always called Ibby, and Adah – the register gets it wrong, with Ada – they followed their father James in going to Logie, a school where everybody still knew each other.

Drumine had been home to many generations of Falconers before James, but although she was aware of that as a child, with a family photo hanging on the parlour wall, her house's centuries of history did not loom large. Neither did the war, her father, as a farmer, being in a reserved occupation. And neither, it seems, did the schoolroom at Logie. The main memories of Pat's school day revolve around Drumine: the whistle of the train to Aviemore prompting her to get up and wash at eight o'clock each day, the walk with a crowd of children across the fields at Presley, arriving back home on hot days to sit on the edge of the sink and have margarine rubbed into her sore feet. She can't remember her favourite subject at school and while there were lunches, none stands out. Mr Pratt is remembered as strict, as she accepted he had to be.

Pat was working as a waitress at the Queen's Hotel on the High Street, now the Co Op, when her grandmother died. Her manager rang to refuse her the Saturday off for the funeral, so she chose to throw in the job instead. I'm glad to hear that there was a limit to her acceptance of how things had to be.

Pat will go back to Drumine soon, to see the latest Falconer, her late brother's baby granddaughter, born just before we meet. It's been a while since she was there but she's glad to see it being smartened up and still worked as a farm. And the last time I walked down the track past Drumine, I noticed there were horses in the field.

No: 1343, Kirsty Love, County Cottages.

'Now, when I think about it, I shouldn't have..'

County Cottages • Christina Wright (Love)

As I arrive at the house, I'm imagining what impact the war years would have had on a small child whose dad was away in the army for much of her early life. As we settle down to talk, it's the first question I ask. There's not a moment's hesitation.

'We started getting curry at school! With sultanas in it! I wouldn't touch it, and there was no pudding, so I came home and just collapsed at the door. My mother went up and created merry hell.'

Christina – or Kirsty as she always was, because her granddad called her that – says she was just like other children in those days: she was left to be a child, not troubled by adult worries. She knew her father whenever he came home because she was told who he was by her mother and the war did not mean as much as I'd expected. She thinks her father had been away in Germany but isn't sure. It's not like now, she says, when children know all sorts, like how much money's coming into the house. Adults just didn't share things and children had no need to worry. If it was tough – and it sounds as if it was – then her mother never really let them know.

There were two bedrooms in their house with, once her dad was home, four girls in one bedroom and her parents sharing their room with Kirsty's twin brother David. If you wanted hot water, you had to boil it first; all their clothes were made or knitted at home; the children got home-made toys for Christmas (a doll's pram with a hood, she remembers in particular) and she was twelve before she had a bike, although she spent more time falling off it than staying on. Her father got a car when she was nine or so, and they'd all pile in, but the butcher and the other vans would call at the house, so they never used it for shopping. Dr Bethune would call by if he was in the area and so would the minister. 'Did you believe in God?' 'Sometimes!' she says, but that really wasn't the point. 'We had no choice. We were told to go to Sunday school. You'd come home and change your clothes again, just like after school.'

While foreign foods were finding their way onto the school menu, travel outside Scotland was still a distant prospect for the Wright family. Holidays – not that there seems to have been much time for them – were spent at an auntie's at Strathdon in Aberdeenshire. Kirsty's grandparents lived on a croft at Delnies near Nairn and when her granny died, the family moved to look after her granddad, stooking, lifting tatties and turnips. It makes Kirsty's early life at Logie sound leisurely in comparison. While they were at Logie they'd play in the woods around the house after school, although even there they had to dig tatties for tea.

Until she had her photograph taken for this project, Kirsty had never been back to County Cottages. The family used to drive past sometimes if they were heading south but never stopped. 'You have to know the people, don't you, to call by?'

●

Children might have been left to be children then, but it strikes me that adulthood came suddenly. Kirsty didn't have a favourite subject at school, but she knew she wanted to work with babies. She'd had enough practice, with three little sisters. Kirsty was working in a shoe shop when she left the Academy but got word of work at Leanchoil hospital.

By the time she was sixteen, then, there she was, living in the nurses' quarters and enjoying life. Her parents had moved 70-odd miles away to the Fort Augustus area, her dad working for the hydro, far easier than working a croft and holding down a council job on the roads as well. Kirsty was working on the maternity ward, helping to deliver babies, washing the new-borns, taking them through to their mothers at feeding time, but she never got a qualification. 'That's one thing I regret: I got married instead.' She was nineteen. The regret is not the marriage itself, nor the five babies of her own (four boys and a girl, the reverse of her mother): it's that she was expected to make a choice between being a wife and working at Leanchoil. 'Now, when I think about it, I shouldn't have.'

●

Before I go, we talk a bit about Margaret Gardiner, a child whose name is just below Kirsty and her brother's in the Logie register. She was killed a few days short of her seventh birthday in a farm accident on Altyre. Hitching a lift on a trailer with a friend, she was crushed by the water tank it was carrying when the tractor turned a corner. Rosemary McKenzie, a few years older than Margaret and a few pages before her in the register, escaped unharmed.

I look up the report in the *Forres, Elgin & Nairn Gazette* and notice in the brief and sober account how much our reporting of news has changed. I think about Margaret and the illusion created by the neat ordering of the register, the methodical listing of names deceptively reassuring, suggesting somehow that every child on that list would be offered an equal chance at life.

No: 1406, Jim Calder, Presley.

‘Whenever I dream, whatever it’s about, it’s always at Presley.’

Presley • James Moir Calder

We start in the obvious place. ‘That’s the room I was born in,’ says Jim, pointing to a window looking out across farmland towards the railway line east of Presley. The photo was taken before an extension was added, so the house is smaller than it is now, and the scale of the steadings – which are barely visible from the road today – dominates the picture. They look magnificent but they’d be no use as farm buildings now, says Jim, the doors too narrow for modern machinery.

There were many more Calders at Presley before Jim, back in the dim and distant, as he says, but they first appear in the Logie School register in 1885 with his grandfather George, with another eleven Presley Calders listed before Jim makes an appearance: his father John and his five siblings, then John’s first family of five and, finally, Jim. His mother Annie had wanted him always known as James, as the register has it, until the day a neighbour asked for ‘wee Jamesie’. His mother hated that so Jim it was, from then on.

Looking at the room where he was born is significant because Jim was the last Calder to have grown up at Presley and the last who could have come back but didn’t, breaking that long link with the family. There were other places to go. ‘I had options, I had job offers,’ he says, ‘all of which looked better than being a tenant farmer of a hundred acres in upland Morayshire. But I felt guilty, in a way, because my name was on the lease. If I’d wanted it, I could have had it. I was the only one who could have carried it on, and I chose not to.’

We talk, much more, about the happy start he had in life and the great freedom of his childhood, about the school and the church, where everyone sat in the same place each week, though there was no hint for a visitor of where that might be, and the laird’s family seated in a gallery above the rest of the congregation, looking down. We talk about the landscape: the Fairy Hillock, now topped by a turbine, where Macbeth met the witches

– or so his Uncle Bill would say – and the distinction between what his father called the Toll Road, now the main road, and the farm road from Outlawell to Drumine and Presley, formerly the only route south.

And just as we are done and I am rummaging for my car keys, he says the thing about his dreams. 'I ask other people, 'When you dream, where is it?' And they shrug and say, 'Well, anywhere!' They don't know what I mean. But for me, whenever I dream, whatever it's about, it's always at Presley, it's always there. I knew every corner, every bit of it, in those formative years.'

●

I wonder if there was a certain pressure in being a Calder at Logie School. Jim's grandfather had been important locally, the Parish Registrar and Inspector of Poor in Edinkillie, while all six of his children were big figures too, in one way or another. His uncle Bill – known more formally as Professor Sir William Calder – had the house opposite the farm as his summer residence, being professor of Greek at Edinburgh and, before that, at Manchester. Archaeology was his obsession and he spent long periods in Asia Minor. Isabelle's and Charles' various paths led them to India, while Edith, like William, was an academic. Their brother George was killed in the First World War, and according to the Morayshire Roll of Honour, 'His death, on 25 September 1915 at the battle of Loos, cut short a life marked by rare ability and rich promise.' I'd come to Jim supposing that war might dominate the family story, with two George Macbeth Calders on the Edinkillie memorial, the second one Jim's cousin. I'm pleased that the stories of the ones who survived are the ones most clearly handed down.

Jim says his father John was maybe the cleverest of them all but left university before graduating, to return home to Presley when his father became too ill to run the farm. Did John remember this, I wonder, when his own son Jim had his choice of career to make? Along with the farm, John took over from his father the duties of Registrar, a plaque by the farmhouse door, meaning that Jim's childhood was punctuated by the bereaved of Edinkillie knocking to register a death and by weddings in the front room at Presley, his grandfather's copy of *Graham on Poor Law* still on the family bookcase there. The Calders, says Jim, 'came from a little tenanted farm halfway to the Dava,' had done well and mostly travelled far. If those two things were taken by a child to be linked, then the seed of not staying must already have been sown.

●

Jim's bedroom faced north and had a good view in the summer: as the year wore on, the window would be obscured by ice. Presley was a freezing cold house. The only heating was the Aga in the kitchen, and while the fire in the sitting room would be lit in the evenings, getting from one to the other meant running like hell.

In the mornings in termtime, Jim tells me, he would cross the road to the school with his slate and a bottle of water and cloth to clean it with – others tell me that they'd just spat on theirs – but that's as much as we talk about his classroom life. 'It was expected that I would be in the A stream at secondary school and that I would go to university. It was not a huge pressure, but it was expected that it would happen. And it did.'

The strongest memories are outdoor ones, of botany with Mr Pratt – 'a damn good teacher' – who was a perfect fit for a country school, teaching far more than the standard curriculum. He'd challenge the children to bring in plants and flowers for identification, which was fine at the start of the season but harder as spring turned to summer and the year wore on. With the railway embankment running straight through the middle of Presley, though, the only bit of uncultivated land on the farm, Jim could easily impress his teacher, especially with rarities blown in on trains.

The farm faced the railway as much as the road and the line gave a framework to Jim's days: the passing of the 8.30 train from Dunphail to Forres acting as the signal to him to go home in the evening, the move from steam to diesel marked by the changing sound of the horn. In his early childhood, he recalls steam trains laden with aluminium, planes scrapped at Kinloss or Lossiemouth, struggling up the slope and sometimes blocking the single-track line completely. Cattle would still be carried from Dunphail, where Mr Pozzi (pronounced Posy) was the stationmaster. And people, too, of course, heading away and coming back past Presley (which, while we're on the subject, is pronounced Pres-lie).

•

Jim did his own heading away and coming back too, while studying agriculture at Aberdeen University, keeping his contact with home but gradually moving his focus and most of his friendships east. His father retired just as Jim graduated but, 'I didn't want to do it, I didn't want to farm Presley, I didn't feel it was what I wanted to do with my life. If I could have gone away and worked and come back when I was 40 ... but that wasn't an option.' None of Jim's half-brothers, all old enough to be his father, had wanted to take on the farm; Geordie had been the last one before Jim and he'd taken on Dunphail Garage with his father, later running the bus and then the Post Office. So although it felt as if Jim was the one leaving Presley, they all had, in their way. The pattern of farming was changing, and Presley's land was divided among the tenants to either side. 'I think father had realised that I would do something else.' He had a very successful career as an agricultural adviser and if he visits now, it feels as if he's an onlooker. Across the road is a more solid family regret: Presley Cottage, as it was called then. It had been built by Jim's grandfather and, an impressive house, had never really been a cottage. It was sold out of the family, who feared that – what with that crack in the chimney – it would surely be a millstone around their necks.

Just before I leave, Jim recalls an evening from his teenage years, when he was fishing on the Divie. There was a pattern to his life then: on dry evenings he'd go shooting, on wet evenings he'd fish. He'd be after brown trout but of course he couldn't help it if a grilse made its way onto his hook now and then. A plane came low overhead, Sir Hector Laing flying home to Dunphail and keeping an eye on his salmon as he landed his plane at Relugas Mains. (He'd later go for less bumpy landings at Mundole.) Half an hour later, as Jim knew he would, along came the keeper to tell him to get off.

This idea of an aerial view, of looking down on familiar places from a different angle, is how Jim's stories have made me feel. It's as if he has laid out a relief map, with contours and textures, colours and shading: the school, the station, the fields, the church, the railway line, viaduct, river and road. And there, always at the very centre of it all, right at the heart, stands Presley.

No: 1561, Sandi Palmer, Woodhead.

'You never used to see the sides of the road for snow..'

Woodhead • Sheila Morrison and Alexandra E. Morrison (Palmer)

As these stories inch closer to us in time, the links between the names in the Logie register and the school of today become more concrete. Joe and Matthew, two of the present pupils, can find their great-great-grandfather James A. Grant, his children, grandchildren and beyond within its pages. Two of his granddaughters, Sheila Grant Morrison and Sandi Palmer, told me part of the Grant family story.

•

The image conjured up by the words great-great-grandfather is a man in very old age. It's a shock, then, to learn that James A. Grant, the handyman on Logie Estate, was killed in 1935 at the age of 38.

FATALITY AT EARNSIDE – LOGIE ESTATE WORKER KILLED

To-day the funeral takes place in Edinkillie churchyard of Mr James A. Grant, news of whose death on Sunday forenoon caused a painful sensation in the district, where his cheerful, obliging disposition caused him to be so popular. He was known as the "handyman" on the Logie estate of Sir Alexander Grant, and he was "everybody's man," capable with his hands, and always ready to render a kindly service to his neighbours. Sympathy goes out to the occupants of the trim little cottage which stands in the grounds of Logie estate, a greatly bereaved widow and five children.

Mr Grant, who was 38 years of age, had attended the motor cycling races at Lossiemouth on Saturday. On the return journey he visited his brother-in-law, who lives at Earnside. He said good-bye to his sister at 9 p.m. She heard the "hoot" of his motor horn, as he was leaving the service road – and then a crash.

A car struck the cyclist with such terrible force that his leg was broken, his skull and jaw fractured. He was taken to Leanchoil hospital, and died about mid-day. Mr Grant had been employed at Logie since it came into possession of the present proprietor, Sir Alexander Grant.

●

Edith, James' widow, maintained the family's connection with Woodhead, the house described by the paper as the trim little cottage on the estate, making ends meet by taking in as lodgers the French-Canadian lumberjacks who were working locally in the forestry. They had already left their mark on the area, having been brought in to help boost the national timber production in World War One. They'd built a railway below Sluie on which to extract the logs and their distinctive shoulder-height sawing produced stumps clearly distinct from those left by Scottish woodsmen.

The five children left without a father – Edith had been pregnant but lost the sixth after her husband died – were Jim, Peggy, Edith, Jock and Babs, all in the Logie School register, with Edith later becoming the mother of the two women sitting with me now. For Sheila, who went to Logie in 1951 – as entry 1465 in the register – the memories of Woodhead date from the time when she and her family stayed there with their granny, her father away in the RAF. She recalls it as a place of sagging floors, the beds sloping off at an angle beneath narrow coombed ceilings. By the time her younger sister Sandi (Alexandra in the register) remembers the house, the family had moved to Relugas and Woodhead had become a Sunday motorbike ride to see their granny, her father driving with Sandi squeezed behind him, her mother on the back, her brother up front on the petrol tank as they wound their way up past Randolph's Leap.

How people got around then crops up a lot in my conversation with Sheila and Sandi. After the war, motorbikes were the only available transport, the Morrisons also owning a sidecar. They went on to be the first family in Relugas to have a car (and later, in fact, the first to have a television too). There was a bus from Dunphail to take the country folk to Forres, says Sheila, locally known – in a sign of the times – as 'the dummy's bus', the driver being deaf. The journey was clearly an adventure for a child of that time. Sheila paints a vivid picture of coming home to Woodhead, her father back on leave and eager to hear her talk of how the people on the bus had admired her lovely red curls.

The word that springs to mind for Sheila, when I ask her about school, is chilblains: the old-fashioned coal heater was still in place in the classroom. It was neither a happy nor an unhappy time for her: 'You just went in'. The food was always home-made and good, the playtime entertainment, apart from marbles, being to stand on tiptoe at the kitchen window to watch the tatties flying out of the peeler. Mrs Mackenzie might have been pleased to know that Sheila went on to be a school cook too. There was grace before meals – was it 'Thank you for the food we eat, thank you Lord for everything'? – and Mr Pratt made sure you ate it all, some days being harder than others: the diced raw vegetables, the sago, the semolina with jam, the pudding like frogs' eggs, the rhubarb fool and – no persuasion needed – the steamed syrup sponge with custard.

•

For Sandi, the trip to school from Relugas, once the family had settled there, was by Dunc Clark's taxi from the crossroads, but only until the age of eight, when children were deemed old enough to cycle or walk from the village, heading down the brae, over the bridge and up Pitteneask to Logie School. Later, when they went on to Forres Academy, they'd cycle to South Lodge and catch Geordie Calder's bus from there There'd always be a crowd of them heading home, grazing when they could on blaeberries, the stains around their mouths telling the tale of why they'd got home late. In cold weather, the walk was often done in wellies, the snow piled up high to either side of the road, and a bad winter might keep them home for six weeks at a time.

As we talk, Sandi reaches behind me to take from a shelf an inkwell she's found in her garden in Relugas, probably from the old village school and just like the ones that would have been used at Logie. It's good not just to talk but to hold a souvenir of a time long gone and it strikes me how rich this family is in physical reminders of its own past: James was a craftsman rather than a handyman, it seems, and carved with his son Jim the font and minister's chair in Edinkillie church. There's also within the family the horsehair chair from Dunphail House, and the stag's head, carried home on the handlebars of Edith's bike, surplus to requirements when Hector Laing refurbished the place for his new bride Marian. The stag is still called Hector. Edith's sister Peggy was a chambermaid for the Laings: they'd always hold a party for the children and invite the estate workers to family weddings.

Sandi was at Logie School for a very significant changeover: from the era of the Pratts in charge to that of the Macivers, who the register tells us were at the school from 1959 to 1970. Jean Maciver brought a wave of sophistication with her to Dunphail, Sandi still recalling the first time she saw her new teacher with her lipstick and eyeshadow ('She had no family.') She brought French lessons to the school, as well as some lessons in Gaelic mouth music, thanks to the couple's Stornoway roots. That music is still in there somewhere, says Sandi, but it takes a few glassfuls before it comes out.

She leaves me with a mental image of herself walking through the late-night streets of Edinburgh, singing the music of the Western Isles, taught to her in Moray, a souvenir of Logie School.

NEW
ADMISSION
REGISTER

Year 1890 - 190

Successive Number	Date of Admission			Name in Full (Christian and Surname)	If Re-admitted Original Admission Number	Exact Date of Birth			Name and Address of Parent or Guardian		Last School Attended before Entering this School
	Year	Month	Day			Year	Month	Day			
1	344	2	5	81	Christina Noble	344	73	8	2	John Noble	Dunphail	None
2	354	82	3	20	Thomas Robertson		76	8	30	Wm Robertson	N Lodge Dunphail	"
3	384	83	4	18	Mary Duncan		77	5	4	Jas Duncan	Mount Dunphail	"
4	385	83	5	9	Cath Macdonald		77	5	14	Wm Macdonald	G Keeper Logie	"
5	406	84	3	17	Margt Hay		76	12		Robt Hay	B Smith Altyre	"
6	407	84	4	1	Alexander Petrie		77	11	4	Wm Petrie	Belevlair	"
7	410	84	5	12	John Hardie		78	8	18	Geo Hardie	Farmer Trafelo	"
8	420	84	10	14	Alexander Hendry		78	11	20	Alex Hendry	Mason Sluie	"
9	421	84	11	3	Alexander McIntosh		78	4	26	Alex McIntosh	Carnoch	"
10	428	85	4	8	Eliza Henderson		79	2	12	Jas Henderson	Grieve Altyre	"
11	429	85	4	6	Alexr Macdonald		79	8	7	Wm Macdonald	G Keeper Logie	"
12	432	85	4	21	Christina Duncan		79	4	21	Jas Duncan	Mount Dunphail	"
13	433	85	4	28	Fred Robertson		80	3	4	Wm Robertson	N Lodge Dunphail	"
14	436	85	6	8	John Mellis		78	7	20	Wm Mellis	Longlea	"
15	437	85	7	2	Rodk Macbain		81	1	18	Alex McBain	The Ditch	"
16	438	85	7	20	Robt Anderson		78	12	7	Robt Anderson	Dunphail	"
17	439	85	10	27	Wm M Calder		81	7	2	Geo Calder	Farmer Presley	"
18	440	85	11	16	Don Cruickshank		81	5	14	Don Cruickshank	Peathillock	"
19	443	86	3	22	Alfr Anderson		77	10	10	Rev A Anderson	F C Manse	Relugas Soe
20	446	86	6	14	Mary I McIntosh		80	4	29	Alex McIntosh	Carnoch	None
21	449	86	7	6	Janet Duncan		80	11	5	Robt Duncan	Presley	"
22	457	86	10	5	John Kemp		80	1	7	John Kemp	C'man Blairs	"
23	464	87	4	4	Alexander Little		77	7	26	Alex Little	Relugas Ho	Relugas Soe
24	465	87	5	9	John Morrison		81	12	8	John Stewart	S'herd Longlea	None
25	466	87	5	18	Rosella Petrie		80	2	7	Wm Petrie	Belevlair	"
26	467	87	5	30	Anne Macbain		82	12	25	Alex McBain	Ditch	"
27	468	87	6	1	Don Macdonald		82	4	19	Wm Macdonald	Keeper Logie	"
28	470	87	6	6	Robina Anderson		80	2	29	David Anderson	Longlea	"
29	472	87	6	6	James Lauder		81	3	31	Jno Lauder	Lower Sluie	"
30	473	87	6	8	James Millar		80	7	21	Geo Millar	S Fisher do	"
31	474	87	6	9	Cath G Henderson		81	11	22	Jas Henderson	Grieve Altyre	"
32	476	87	7	6	Joseph Shand		82	6	6	Wm Shand	Ramphletts	"
33	477	87	7	12	Alexander Cameron		81	12	16	Geo Cameron	S Fisher L Sluie	"
34	435	87	7	21	Hugh Shand		79	9	21	Wm Shand	Ramphletts	"
35	478	87	10	5	Maggie McDougall		80	3	6	D McDougall	C'man Logie	Strathglass Pu
36	479	87	10	5	Billy McDougall		81	9	21	do	do	do
37	480	87	11	2	M Lily McGlashan		80	12	23	Wm McGlashan	Farmer Muir of Logie	None
38	481	88	4	3	Isabella Calder		83	3	22	Geo Calder	Farmer Presley	"
39	482	88	4	16	Alexander Cairns		80	12	9	Thomas Cairns	Sluie	St Johns Epis. H
40	483	88	4	16	James Cairns		82	9	1	do	do	None
41	484	88	4	19	Anne Kemp		82	3	30	John Kemp	C'man Blairs	"
42	485	88	5	28	Cath McIntosh		82	5	4	Alex Macintosh	Carnoch	"
43	486	88	6	5	Charles Mellis		82	3	20	Wm Mellis	Longlea	"
44	475	88	6	11	Jane Millar		82	7	20	Geo Millar	S Fisher L Sluie	Logie School
45	458	88	12	11	Thos Robertson		82	9	26	Dom Robertson	S Fisher Sluie	None
46	492	89	4	8	John McDougall		83	5	7	D McDougall	Logie	"
47	493	89	4	8	David McDougall		84	8	6	do	do	"
48	494	89	4	18	Wm Petrie		82	10	31	Wm Petrie	Belevlair	"
49	495	89	6	4	Margt Innes		81	10	24	Innes	C Hall Rafford	Liverpool H'town
50	497	89	6	12	Wm Cruickshank		84	9	2	Don Cruickshank	Peathillock	None

Notes by Teacher and Signatures of School Managers with date of visit.

WHETHER EXEMPTION FROM RELIGIOUS INSTRUCTION CLAIMED	The highest standard in which he was there presented and the results of his last EXAMINATION				Class into which admitted	Showing the Successive Standards in which presented in this School, with date and result of examination						Showing the Specific Subjects in which he was presented in his LAST and in THIS School.																EXACT DATE OF LEAVING			CAUSE OF LEAVING
												STANDARD V		STANDARD VI		STANDARD Ex. VI		STANDARD Ex. Ex. VI												
	St.d	R.	W.	A.		I	II	III	IV	V	VI	No. of Subject	Stage	No. of Subject	Stage	No. of Subject	Stage	No. of Subject	Stage	No. of Subject	Stage	No. of Subject	Stage	No. of Subject	Stage	Year	Month	Day	
No																										90	5	6	Education finished
																									90	4	2	Gone to Relugas School
																									90	4	3	Schooling finished
																									90	4	11	do.
																									90	4	3	do
																									90	5	16	Gone to Dunphail School
																									90	5	2	do Relugas "
																									22	8	90	Gone to Rafford
																									90	5	2	Gone to Relugas School
																												Gone to Dunphail School.
																									90	4	11	Schooling finished
																									90	5	2	Schooling finished
																									90	5	16	Gone to Dunphail School
																									22	8	90	Gone to Rafford
																									90	5	16	Gone to Dunphail School
																									90	6	11	Gone to live in Forres

Successive Number	Date of Admission — Year	Month	Day	Name in Full Christian and Surname	If Re-admitted Original Admission Number	Exact Date of Birth — Year	Month	Day	Name and Address of Parent or Guardian		Last School Attended before entering this school
51	498	89	7	2	Maggie Macdonald		82	6	5	Wm Macdonald	G Keeper Logie	None
52	499	89	7	2	Hugh Anderson		83	10	11	Robt Anderson	Dunphail	"
53	500	89	10	7	William Hendry		78	6	8	Alex Hendry	Sluie	Forres Pub
54	417	89	6	19	Colin Macrae		78	5	23	Colin Macrae	Drumine	Logie
55	501	89	10	31	Isa Macrae		83	9	12	do	do	None
56	387	89	5	30	Wm Macdonald		76	7	29	John McDonald	Ditch	Logie
57	377	89	11	26	Jessie Millar		76	10	9	Geo Millar	Store Sluie	do
58	412	89	12	2	George Millar		78	7	25	do	do	do
59	403	89	12	2	Wm Anderson		76	7	15	Robt Anderson	Dunphail	do
60	356	89	12	10	John Shand		76	8	4	Wm Shand	Ramphlets	do
61	302	89	12	16	Geo Robertson		73	8	9	Wm Robertson	N Lodge Dunphail	do
62	359	90	1	13	Charles Inch		76	9	6	Wm Inch	Feus Logie	do
63	391	90	2	12	Margt Duncan		78	5		Robt Duncan	Presley	do
64	502	17	3	90	Jane Hendry		83	2	8	Alex Hendry	Mason Sluie	Infant Sch Forr
65	503	14	4	"	George Grigor		84	6	7	Alex Grigor	Drumine	None
66	504	5	5	"	William Duncan		84	9	17	Robert Duncan	Presley	"
67	505	"	"	"	William Lander		84	4	25	James Lander	Lower Sluie	"
68	506	"	"	"	Charles Calder		83	12	3	George Calder	Presley	"
69	507	12	"	"	James Murray		84	4	7	Murray	Ardoch	"
70	508	16	6	"	Wilhelmina Kemp		84	4	2	John Kemp	C'man Blairs	"
71	499	90	10	14	John Grant		81	8	10	Mrs Grant	Craighead Altyre	Half Davoch
72	477	90	11	19	John McIntosh		84	1	6	Mrs Duncan		Dunphail
73	513	90	12	8	James McIntosh		76	4	2	Wm McIntosh	Regal	Forres Pub
74	514	"	"	"	John Duncan		76	1	23	James Duncan	"	Dunphail
75	515	91	1	5	Alex McIntosh	421	78	4	21	Alex McIntosh	Carnock	Logie
76	516	90	12	1	John Mellis	436	78	7	20	William Mellis	Longley	"
77	517	91	1	6	John Cruickshank		77	12	9	Donald Cruickshank	Reathillock	Relugas
78	538	91	1	7	Robert Anderson	438	78	12	7	Robert Anderson	Dunphail	Logie
	514				William Anderson	403	76	7	15	"	"	"
	515	91	4	7	James Allan		78	8	6	William Allan	Tullyglens	Relugas
	516	"	"	"	Jeanie Allan		76	12	11	"	"	"
	517	"	"	"	Maggie Allan		79	10	1	"	"	"
	518	"	"	"	William Johnston		79	1	10	William Johnston	Oikyorn	Dunphail
	519	"	"	"	Robert Murray Jas		77	5	14	Robert Murray	Forres Lodge Altyre	Forres
	520	"	"	"	John Murray		81	12	19	"	"	"
	521	"	"	"	Robert Murray Jas		85	10	10	James Murray	Oakfield	None
	522	"	6		Bella McIntosh		84	10	14	Alexander McIntosh	Carnock	"
	523	91	7	30	Robert Fraser		85	6	19	Robert Fraser	Rose Cottage	"
	524	91	8	3	John Miller		84	10	25	George Miller	Sluie	"
	525	91	10	12	John Calder		86	12	5	George Calder	Presley	
	526	91	10	19	John Johnstone		8	4	14	William Johnstone	Oikyorn	Dunphail
	527	91	10	19	Jessie Johnstone		84	6	4	"	"	
	528	91	12	8	Alexander D. McKenzie		84	6	28	Hugh McKenzie	Sluie	Dallas
	529	92	2	15	Alex. Campbell		83	4	4	Malcolm Campbell	Sluie	Kinloss
	530	"	"	16	Jessie Cameron		79	10	22	William Cameron	Dunphail	Dunphail
	531	"	"	"	William Cameron		83	1	9	"	"	
	532	92	4	11	William Forrest		86	12	30	William Mellis	Longley	None
	533	92	4	19	Nellie Campbell		87	4	20	Malcolm Campbell	Sluie	Kinloss
	534	92	5	2	Catherine N. Anderson		85	12	6	Robert Anderson	Carnock	None

Notes by Teacher and Signatures of School Managers with date of visit.

J. Macleod H.M.

14/90

WHETHER EXEMPTION FROM RELIGIOUS INSTRUCTION IS CLAIMED	The highest standard in which he was there presented, and the results of his last EXAMINATION				Class into which admitted	Showing the Successive Standards in which presented in this School, with date and result of examination.						Showing the Specific Subjects in which he was presented in his LAST and in THIS School.																				EXACT DATE OF LEAVING			CAUSE OF LEAVING.
	Std	R.	W.	A.		I.	II.	III.	IV.	V.	VI.																				Year	Month	Day	
//																														90	4	11	Gone to live in Forres
//																																	
//																																	
//																														90	5	16	Gone to Service
//																														90	5	2	Gone to Work
//																														90	4	2	do
//																														90	3	28	do
//																														90	4	2	do
//																																	Schooling finished —
//																																	
//	III																																	
6	None																																	Gone to work.
//	VI																																	Intends going into Railway Work.
//	V																																	Gone to work.
//																																		Gone to work for summer
//																																		Gone to work at home.
//																																	
//	VI																																	Left for work.
//																																		Do Do
//	III																																	Do Do
//	V																																	Do Do
//	V																																	Gone to Rafford.
//	III																																	Expelled. Insubordination
//	0																																	
//	//																																	
//	//																																	
//	//																																	Gone to Gordon's Coll. Abdn
//	II																																	Schooling finished
//	0																																	
//	//																																	
	I																																	
	II																																	
	0																																	
	III																																	

Successive Number	Date of Admission or Re-admission			Name in Full (Christian and Surname)	If Re-admitted Original Admission Number	Exact Date of Birth			Name and Address of Parent or Guardian	Last School Attended Before Entering This School
	Year	Month	Day			Year	Month	Day		
535	92	5	2	Jessie McDougall		87	8	29	David McDougall	Coachman Logie	None
536	92	5	24	Nellie Hendry		87	4		McHendry	Sluie	"
537	"	"	25	Jessie Kemp		86	10	9	John Kemp	Blairs Farm	"
538	"	"		Annie Clark		81	9	20	Alexander Clark	School Cottage Logie	Half Davoch
539	"	"		Nellie Clark		87	2	19	" "	"	" "
540	"	"		Robert C Clark		84	12	10	" "	"	" "
541	"	"		Maggie Clark		80	3	15	" "	" "	" "
542	92	6	6	Nellie Allan		81	10	18	William Allan	Torchrisk	Relugas
543	"	"		Jessie Allan		86 84	3 2	10 22	" "		"
544	"	"		William Allan		84	2	22	" "		"
545	"	"		Janet S Grigor		86	9	10	Alexander Grigor	Dykeside	None
546	92	10	5	Robert Rands		80	6	16	Robert Strast	Pointsman Dunphail	Dunphail Pub.
547	92	11	9	Donald Cameron					Donald Cameron	Presley	None
548	92	12	7	Janet Clark		78	7	31	Alexander Clark	School Cottage Logie	Half Davoch
549	93	1	10	Mary A F Robertson		82	1	15	Mrs Robertson	Relugas	Relugas
550	93	1	10	William McHattie		83	3	26	Alexander McHattie	Do	Do.
551	94	3	6	Daisy Jenkins		81	11	5	Mrs Jenkins	Relugas Cottage	Do.
552	93	4	3	Willie R Watt		89	4	27	John Watt	Relugas	Do.
553	"	"		Norman McHattie		86	6	11	Alexander McHattie		
554	"	"	4	Jessie Kemp		86	7	5	John Kemp	Blairs Farm	Logie
555	"	"	10	Annie Hay		87	9	18	Robert Hay	B.Smith Altyre	None
556	"	"	12	Henry C Cruickshank		88	5	25	Donald Cruickshank	Peat hillocks	"
557	"	5	1	John Allan		88	4	26	Wm Allan	Torchrisk	"
558	"	"	2	Jessie Mackenzie		86	5	24	Mrs Paxton	Relugas	Relugas
559	"	"	8	Mary Ann Cameron		87	10	12	Wm Cameron	Dunphail Station	None
560	93	5	30	Jacobina Macbain		82	4	18	Wm McBain	Blairs Farm	Dunphail
561	93	5	31	William Macbain		85	9	20			"
562	"	6	6	Colin Mackenzie		88	4	20	Hugh McKenzie	Sluie	None
563	"	6	13	William Ross		88	8	26	William Ross	Ditch	"
564	"	6	28	Hugh Macbain		80	10	12			
565	93	9	25	Jeannie Ferras					Mrs Jenkins	Relugas Cottage	
566	"	"		William Gourlay		80	12	20	John Gourlay	Relugas Farm	Raining's Sch. Inverness
567	"	"	29	Charles Eddie		84	2	17	George Eddie	Old Blairs	Forres Pub.
568	"	"		James Eddie		86	7	2	" "	"	
569	"	10	16	Murdo Macrae		81	3	7	Mrs Macrae	Broadshaw	Conicavel
570	"	12	11	James Clark		82	1	9	William L Clark	Overseer Blairs Farm	
571	"	"		Charles Clark		84	10	23			
572	"	"		Bella Clark		87	8	28			
573	93	4	12	Donald Matheson		87	6	24	Hugh Matheson	Relugas	
574	94	2	8	Catto Campbell		87	8	8	Malcolm Campbell	Sluie	
575	94	3	26	Janet Garrow		88			Mrs Garrow	Hillockhead	
576	94	3	26	Lizzie Mackenzie		88	10	12	Mrs Fraser	Blackloch	
577	94	3	28	Christina McLennan		89	6	29	M McLennan	Logie	
578				Maggie Ormiston		89	-				
579	94	4	16	James Fraser		81	9	6	John Gourlay	Relugas	
580	"	"		Madeline J Miller		88	3	23	Geo Miller	Sluie	
581	"	6	4	Donald McIntosh		88	8	18	Alex McIntosh	Carnock	
582	"	6	11	Katie McIntosh (a)		88	11	16	James McIntosh	Blairs Farm	
583	"	6	18	Lizzie Hay		89	2	10	Robert Hay	Altyre Smith	
584	"	"	26	Maggie Taylor		81	12	10	George Taylor	Auchagavin	Dulsie Bridge

Notes by Teacher and Signatures of School Managers with date of visit.

Macleod H M 19.3.94

WHETHER EXEMPTION FROM RELIGIOUS INSTRUCTION IS CLAIMED	The highest standard in which he was there presented, and the results of his last EXAMINATION				Class into which admitted	Showing the Successive Standards in which presented in this School, with date and result of examination.						Showing the Specific Subjects in which he was presented in his LAST and in THIS School.																			EXACT DATE OF LEAVING			CAUSE OF LEAVING.
	St?	R.	W.	A.		I.	II.	III.	IV.	V	VI	STANDARD V		STANDARD VI		STANDARD Ex.VI		STANDARD Ex.Ex.VI										Year	Month	Day	
												N? of Subject	Stage	N? of Subject	Stage	N? of Subject	Stage	N? of Subject	Stage												
No																															Schooling finished
"																															Removed to Forres
"																															"
"																															Schooling finished
"																															Work as P.T.
"																															Schooling finished
																															P.T. in this school.
																															Schooling finished
																															Do Do
																															Do Do.
																															Schooling finished
																															Do Do.
																															Removed to Ardclach.
																															Schooling finished
																															Removed to Forres
																															Gone to Work
																															Removed to Forres
																															Schooling finished
																															Do Do.
																															Removed to Forres.
																															Schooling finished
																															Do Do
																															Do Do.
																															Left the district
																															Schooling finished
																															Removed to Rafford
																															Schooling finished
																															Do Do
																															Do Do
																															Do Do
																															Removed to Forres
																															Left the district
																															Do Do
																															Schooling finished.
																															Left the district
																															Do Do
																															Do Do
																															Gone to work

Successive Number (on admission or re-admission)	Date of Admission or Re-admission (Year)	(Month)	(Day)	Name in Full Christian and Surname	If Re-admitted Original Admission Number	Exact Date of Birth (Year)	(Month)	(Day)	Name and Address of Parent or Guardian		Last School Attended Before Entering This School
585	94	6	26	Marianne Taylor		84	10	25	George Taylor	Auchnagairn	Dulsie Bridge
586	"	"	"	Hilda Taylor		86	12	1	"	—	—
587	"	"	"	George Taylor		89	4	4	"	—	—
588	"	7	3	Simon Grant		62			John Grant	Woodside	Half Davoch
589	"	9	25	William Anderson		86	5	24	Robert Anderson	Altyre Lodge	Moyness
590	"	"	"	Robert Anderson		88	2	4	" "		"
591	"	"	"	John A. Grigor		89	5	29	Alexr. Grigor	Dykeside	none
592	"	"	"	James Anderson		88	5	29	Robert Anderson	Carnock	"
593	"	10	—	George Campbell		89	3	4	Malcolm Campbell	Sluie	"
594	95	3	14	John B. Russell		90	9	2	William Russell	Logie Schoolho.	"
595	"	3	12	Alexander Taylor		83	8	1	George Taylor	Auchnagairn	Dulsie Bridge
596	"	"	25	Lizzie Lauder		89	4	10	James Lauder	Sluie	none
597	"	"	"	John Piercy		89	8	22	Adam R. Piercy	"	"
598	"	"	27	Wm J. R. Gair		88	4	29	Alexr. Gair	Craigroy	Half Davoch
599	"	4	12	R. J. D. McKenzie		89	3	29	Hugh McKenzie	Sluie	none
600	"	"	4	Charles Kemp		"	6	29	John Kemp	Blairs Farm	none
601	"	"	8	John Tulloch		83	5	12	Wm Bogg	Longlea	Forres
602	"	"	"	Robert Russell		"	"	18	Wm Russell	Chash Chu	Half Davoch
603	"	"	"	Charles Russell		85	—	25	"		"
604	"	"	9	Lewis Fraser		82	5	17	F. Fraser	Phorp	"
605	"	"	23	Hugh Mathieson		89	3	9	Hugh Mathieson	Relugas	none
606	"	6	3	Jessie Duncan						Blairs	Burgie
607	"	"	5	David McLean		83	3	20	Hector McLean	Relugas	Forres
608	"	"	"	Annie Eddie		88	7	29	George Eddie	Blairs Farm	none
609	"	6	24	James Clark		88	1	8	James Clark	Gardener Logie	West End Elgin
610	"	10	1	Mina McDonald		90	4	14	Wm McDonald	Gamekeeper Relugas	none
611	"	"	"	Maggie McDonald	51	84	6	5	"		Forres
612	"	"	3	John McKenzie		89	7	7	Donald McKenzie	Altyre	Half Davoch
613	"	"	"	Alexander McKenzie		87	5	28	"		"
614	"	"	"	Annie McKenzie		84	2	24	"		"
615	"	11	12	Alexander McIntosh		80	9	3	James McIntosh	Gamekeeper Dunphail	Dunphail
616	"	"	25	Chrissie Clark		91	9	11	Alexander Clark	Road Contractor Logie	none
617	"	"	"	Johnina McLennan		91	4	27	Wm McLennan	Gamekeeper Logie	"
618	96			John Hendry		82	8	27	James Hendry	Farmer Airdrie	Glenferness
619	96	3	24	William Davidson		84	1	17	Wm Davidson	Craigroy	Half Davoch
620	"	"	"	Peter Davidson		85	11	30	" "		"
621	"	"	"	Janet Davidson		87	11	27	" "		"
623	"	"	"	James McBain		84	11	2	Mrs Macbain	Auldhuisack	"
624	"	"	"	Mary A. Paul		86	9	5	Mrs Garrow	Craigroy	"
625	"	6	1	George Calder		91	5	29			none
626	"	"	"	Duncan McLennan		92	11	30			"
627	"	"	2	Bella Hay		91	2	25			"
628	"	"	9	Katie Piercy		91	2	1			"
629	"	"	"	Lizzie Miller		90	12	11	George Miller	Sluie	"
630	"	"	"	Jessie Ann Ross		90	7	24			"
631	"	"	15	James Anderson (a)		88	3	17	James Anderson	Cuthavell	Forres Pub.
632	"	"	"	Jane Ann Anderson		89	11	23	"		"
633	"	"	"	Maggie Ann Inch		91	3	22	Wm Inch	Parkhead	none
634	"	7	14	Minnie Cameron		88	10	4	Wm Cameron	Dunphail	none
635	"	9	28	Bruce A. Russell		92	2	12	Wm Russell	Logie Schoolho.	none

Notes by Teacher and Signatures of School Managers with date of visit

J. Macleod H.M.
5.3.95

WHETHER EXEMPTION FROM RELIGIOUS INSTRUCTION IS CLAIMED	The highest standard in which he was there presented, and the results of his last EXAMINATION.				Class into which admitted	Showing the Successive Standards in which presented in this School, with date and result of examination.						Showing the Specific Subjects in which he was presented in his LAST and in THIS School.																		EXACT DATE OF LEAVING			CAUSE OF LEAVING.
	St.	R.	W.	A.		I.	II.	III.	IV.	V	VI	STANDARD V		STANDARD VI		STANDARD Ex. VI.		STANDARD Ex. Ex. VI.										Year	Month	Day	

J. Macleod H.M.
10.3.97

Successive Number (on admission or re-admission)	Date of Admission or Re-admission			Name in Full Christian and Surname	If Re-admitted Original Admission Number	Exact Date of Birth			Name and Address of Parent or Guardian.		Last School Attended Before Entering This School
	Year	Month	Day			Year	Month	Day			
636	96	10	5	Nellie Macdonald		90	5	22	Dnald McDonald	Sluie	None
637	"	"	"	Willie Fraser		90	3	28	James Fraser	Do	Do
638	"	"	2	Duncan Cameron							
639	"	11	23	Andrew Clark		90	11	6	William Clark	Blairs Farm	None
640	"	12	14	William Whyte		84	3	6	Jas Anderson	Outlawwell	Findhorn
641	97	1	4	Simon Grant	588				John Grant	Woodside	
642	97	4	26	William Douglas		91	8	4	Mrs McKenzie	Presley	None
643	"	5	4	Ethel Campbell		91	11	24	Malcolm Campbell	Sluie	Do
644	"	4	4	William Watt	552	87	4	27	Robert O. Watt	Relugas	Relugas
645	"	"	"	Norman McHattie	553	86	6	11	Alex. McHattie	Do	Do
646	"	"	"	James Muirhead		86	10	31	John Muirhead	Culmony	Do
647	"	"	"	George Taylor	587	89	4	7	George Taylor	Auchnagairn	Do
648	"	5	"	Katie Campbell	574	87	3	8	Malcolm Campbell	Sluie	East End Elgin
649	"	"	24	Mary R. Paul	6011	86	9	5	John Garrow	Woodhead	Dingwall Academy
650	"	"	"	Jessie McKenzie	558	88	5	24	Wm Allan	Torchroisk	Relugas
651	"	6	7	Simon Fraser		91	6	11	James Fraser	Sluie	None
652	"	"	9	Hugh Mackenzie		91	7	28	Hugh Mackenzie	Do	Do
653	"	12	6	Alexander Clark		93	11	12	Alexander Clark	School Cottage	Do
654	"	12	20	Alexander McKenzie (c)		88	1	16	John Garrow	Woodhead	Kintessack
655	"	"	"	James McKenzie		89	2	9	Do Do	Do	Do
656	"	"	"	Maggie McKenzie		90	1	27	Do Do	Do	Do
657	"	"	14	William Russell		93	3	31	Wm Russell	Logie School	None
658				Wm McHattie	550	83	3	26			
659	98	3	14	Donald McBain		86	11	11	Mrs McBain	Auldishack	Half Davoch
660	"	"	"	John Rackson		92	2	2	Mrs McBain	The Ditch	None
661	"	"	15	Lizzie Stewart		88	11	4	Mrs Stewart	Longley	Gorgie Pub.
662	"	"	"	Annie Hay	555	87	9	18	Robert Hay	Altyre Smithy	Logie
663	"	"	"	John McStephen		88	8	10			Half Davoch
664	"	"	21	Nellie Ross		92	9	7	William Ross	Muir of Sluie	None
665	"	"	"	Andrew Don McDougall		93	6	3	Dav McDougall	Logie Stable	"
666	"	"	"	Wm Alex McBain		91	7	14	Wm Cameron	Station Houses	"
667	"	4	4	Wm Mackay Piercy		92	10	10	Adam Piercy	Sluie	"
668	"	"	7	Bella Mackenzie		93	2	23	Donald McKenzie	Woodhead	"
669	"	"	11	Alexander Anderson		92	5	9	James Anderson	Outlawwell	"
670	"	"	18	William Kemp		91	10	14	John Kemp	Blairs Farm	"
671	"	4	25	Lachlan Nicol		86	7	29	Lachlan Nicol	Sleighhillock	Half Davoch
672	"	"	"	Ina Taylor		92	5	7	George Taylor	Auchnagairn	None
673	"	"	"	Maggie Macdonald					John McDonald	Ditch	"
674	"	6	13	John Ross		89	6	14	John Ross	Moor of Sluie	Forres Pub.
675	"	"	"	Robert Allan		93	1	8	Wm Allan	Torchroisk	None
676	99	4	3	Mary Gollan		93	4		John Henderson	Muir of Logie	"
677	"	"	"	Edith Calder		93	4	29	George McCalder	Presley	"
678	"	"	4	Robina Hay					Robert Hay	Altyre Smithy	"
679	"	"	12	Lizzie Cameron		93	12	12	Wm Nellis	Longlea	"
680	"	5	9	Donald Matheson	573	87	6	24	Hugh Matheson	Relugas	Relugas
681	"	"	"	Mary C Clark					William Clark	Altyre	None
682	"	6	"	Ella Miller		93	8	26	Mrs Miller	Sluie	"
683	"	7	11	Alex McKenzie	613	87	5	28	Don McKenzie	Altyre	Rafford
684	"	"	"	John McKenzie	612	89	7	7	"	"	Do
685	"	"	"	Donald McKenzie							Do

Notes by Teacher and Signatures of School Managers with date of visit.

J. Macleod H.M.
7.3.98

WHETHER EXEMPTION FROM RELIGIOUS INSTRUCTION IS CLAIMED	The highest standard in which he was there presented, and the results of his last EXAMINATION.				Class into which admitted	Showing the Successive Standards in which presented in this School, with date and result of examination.						Showing the Specific Subjects in which he was presented in his LAST and in THIS School.																		EXACT DATE OF LEAVING			CAUSE OF LEAVING.
	Std	R.	W.	A.		I	II.	III.	IV	V	VI	STANDARD V			STANDARD VI			STANDARD Ex VI			STANDARD Ex. Ex. VI			Year	Month	Day	

SUCCESSIVE NUMBER (ON ADMISSION OR RE-ADMISSION)	DATE OF ADMISSION OR RE-ADMISSION			NAME IN FULL CHRISTIAN AND SURNAME	IF RE-ADMITTED ORIGINAL ADMISSION NUMBER	EXACT DATE OF BIRTH			NAME AND ADDRESS OF PARENT OR GUARDIAN.		LAST SCHOOL ATTENDED BEFORE ENTERING THIS SCHOOL
	Year	Month	Day			Year	Month	Day			
686	99	4	16	Emily McLennan		95	3	23	Wm McLennan	Logie	None
687	"	9	26	James M. Russell		94	7	9	Wm Russell	Logie School	"
688	"	"	"	Alex. Campbell		88	2	15	Wilson Campbell	Cothall	Half Davock
689	"	"	"	John Campbell		92	3	14	" "	"	" "
690	"	"	"	Maggie Campbell		89	12	24	"	"	" "
691	"	10	5	Johanna Paul		59	3	6	John Paul	Auchnagairn	Elgin East End
692	"	11	27	Janet Hendry		89	9	1	Jas Anderson	Outlaw well	Forres Pub.
693	"	12	11	Robert Clark	540				Alex Clark	School Cottage	Logie "
694	1900	8	1	James Murray	507				James Murray	Oakfield	" "
695	"	"	"	William Hendry		88	1	11	Mrs Garrow	Aittlockhead	Forres. Pub.
696	"	4	10	William Beattie		94	6		" "	Woodhead	"
697	"	5	2	Hugh Matheson	105	89	3	9	Hugh Matheson	Relugas	Relugas.
698	"	"	28	Ella Ross		94	10	25	Wm Ross	Sluie	None.
699	"	6	15	John Grant		94	5	23	Mrs Grant	Woodside	—
700				Thomas O'Brien		87	12	-	Mr Geo Calder	Presle	Burghead. Pub.
701	"	11	13	Alex. McBain					John McBain	Ditch	none
702	01	3	18	William McBean		88	8	30	Hugh McBean	Preens	Half Davock
703	"	"	25	David J. Grant		89	3	2	John Grant	Woodside	" "
704	"	4	8	Lizzie J. Murray		95	8	2	James Murray	Oakfield Cottage	None
705	"	5	6	John Matheson		91	3	5	Hugh Matheson	Relugas	Relugas
706	"	"	7	Don Matheson		91	2	23	Mrs Matheson Sr.	Do.	Do.
707	"	4	10	Alexander Matheson		92	12	9	Hugh Matheson	Do.	Do.
708	"	5	28	Maggie Williamson		95	6	25	Geo Williamson	Drummine	none
709	"	6	3	David Munro		92	6	5	Alex. Munro	Ditch	Dunphail
710	"	"	"	Elsie Munro		93	12	14	Do Do	Do.	Do.
711	"	"	4	John Stewart		90	5	2	Evan McBain	Do	Forres.
712	"	"	5	Alex Mackay		40	5	17	Don. McKay	Auldushaack	Half Davock
713	"	"	5	Malcolm McBain		97	1	9	Evan McBain	Ditch	none
714	"	6	17	Evan McBain		95	5	20			Forres
715	"	6	10	Jessie Munro		96	2	21	Alexander Munro	Mosside	none
716	"	9	24	Anabella Clark		96	12		James Clark	Logie Gardens	"
717	"	"	"	Bella King		92	2	28	Mrs Holmes	Minr of Sluie	St Johns E. Forres.
718	"	10	7	Roderick McLennan		89	5	13	Kenneth McLennan	Relugas	Col. Campbell. Auldcastle
719	"	4	14	Maggie Piercy		94	11	3	Adam Piercy	Sluie	none
720	02	3	31	Jane McIntosh		96	7	3	Wm McIntosh	Blackloch	"
721	02	3	31	William Robertson		94	11	2	Mrs Robertson	Delevear	Dunphail
722	"	"	"	Bessie Robertson		96	1	12	"	"	"
723	"	"	"	Alexander McIntosh		"	9	7	Alex McIntosh	Carnock	none
724	"	6	25	Archd S Ross		"	11	1	Archd Ross	Logie Gardens	"
725	"	"	27	Bella McTavish		"	"	22	John McTavish	Bt Smith Carnock	"
726	"	12	13	John Davidson		"	5	12	George Davidson	Dunphail G.S.	Feness
727	03	3	12	Jane Sutherland		90	7		A Sutherland	Ditch	Nairn
728	"	"	"	John McLennan		97	11	5	W. McLennan	Logie Lodge	none
729	"	"	"	Peter McLennan		"	"	"	"	"	"
730	"	"	14	William Forbes		"	7	29	Andrew Forbes	Ditch	"
731	"	"	"	John Forbes		99	1	15	"	"	"
732	03	3	16	Mary Watt		93	5	18	John Watt	Relugas	Relugas
733	03	3	23	John McTavish		98	7	17	John McTavish	Bt Smith Carnock	none
734	"	"	"	Roderick Forsyth					Forsyth	Relugas	Relugas
735	"	3	30	Ronald Murray		97	10	1	James Murray	Oakfield	none

Notes by Teacher and Signatures of School Managers with date of visit.

WHETHER [EXEMP]TION FROM [R]ELIGIOUS [IN]STRUCTION [IS] CLAIMED	The highest standard in which he was there presented, and the results of his last EXAMINATION				Class into which admitted	Showing the Successive Standards in which presented in this School, with date and result of examination.						Showing the Specific Subjects in which he was presented in his LAST and in THIS School.																		EXACT DATE OF LEAVING			CAUSE OF LEAVING.
												STANDARD V		STANDARD VI		STANDARD Ex VI		STANDARD Ex Ex VI														
	St.	R.	W.	A.		I.	II.	III.	IV.	V	VI	Nr of Subject	Stage	Nr of Subject	Stage	Nr of Subject	Stage	Nr of Subject	Stage	Nr of Subject	Stage	Nr of Subject	Stage	Nr of Subject	Stage	Nr of Subject	Stage	Year	Month	Day	

SUCCESSIVE NUMBER (on admission or re-admission)	DATE OF ADMISSION (or re-admission)			NAME IN FULL CHRISTIAN AND SURNAME	IF RE-ADMITTED ORIGINAL ADMISSION NUMBER	EXACT DATE OF BIRTH			NAME AND ADDRESS OF PARENT OR GUARDIAN		LAST SCHOOL ATTENDED BEFORE ENTERING THIS SCHOOL
	Year	Month	Day			Year	Month	Day			
736	03	3	30	John Ross					Alex Ross	Coulmony Gdns	Relugas
737	"	"	"	Alexandra Ross					"	"	"
738	"	4	28	Jessie A McLean	97	11	19	Robt Anderson	Longlea	none
739	"	5	5	James McIntosh	97	11	9	Wm McIntosh	Blacklock	
740	"	"	"	George McIntosh	99	2	11			"
741	"	6	30	Mary Ellen Davidson	98	2	1	Geo Davidson	Mosside	
742	04	2	12	Malcolm Campbell	90	11	2	Wm McLennan	Logie Lodge	Dingwall Academy
743	"	"	"	Kenneth A Campbell	92	8	1	do	Do	Do
744	"	3	1	Maggie Geddes						
745	"	"	28	Gladys Ross	98	12	31	Archibald Ross	Logie Gardens	None
746	"	4	11	William Miller	92	1	6			
747	"	"	12	Stewart Innes Russell	98	10	23	William Russell	Logie Schoolhouse	None
748	"	"	18	James Ross	98	10	4	James Ross	Upper Sluie	"
749	"	"	"	Mabel Robertson	C98	9	13	Wm Robertson	Bellevlair	"
750	"	"	20	Bessie Piery	98	5	29	Adam Piery	Lower Sluie	"
751	"	"	26	James Fraser	"	9	10	James Fraser	Upper Sluie	"
752	"	5	2	John O. Watt	95	4	4	John Watt	Relugas	Relugas
753	"	6	1	John Cruickshank	94	8	28	James Cruickshank	Regal	Dunphail
754	"	"	"	Bessie Cruickshank	91	8	24	" "	"	"
755	"	"	6	Donald McPherson						
756	"	"	"	Alex McPherson						
757	"	"	"	James McPherson						
758	"	"	13	Geo A Logie	97	5	30	Mrs Logie	Sluie Lodge	Conicavel
759	05	2	21	Annie Cattanach	43	12	3	John Cattanach	Coulmony Lodge	Relugas
760	"	"	"	Alexander Cattanach	95	4	11			
761	"	4	17	Maggie McTavish	99	8	10	John McTavish	Carnach	None
762	"	5	2	Catherine Ross	00	10	5	Archibald Ross	Logie Gardens	"
763	"	"	8	Jeannie Petrie	00	2	15	John Petrie	Ardoch	"
764	"	"	"	John Wight	01	2	9	William Wight	Mosside	"
765	"	"	"	Katie Wight	99	12	16	"	"	"
766	"	"	"	Ella Robertson	00	1	28	William Robertson	Carnock	"
767	"	"	"	Robert Anderson	00	8	26	William Mellis	Longley	"
768	06	4	3	Mary Murray	01	2	25	James Murray	Oakfield	"
769	"	"	11	Bella Piery	00	4	6	Adam Piery	Sluie Mains	"
770	"	"	9	Georgina Forbes	01	5	7	Andrew Forbes	Ditch	"
771	"	"	30	Jean Falconer	00	11	23	James Falconer	Drummuie	"
772	"	"	"	Donald McBean	00	11	4			"
773	"	5	7	George Williamson	00	3	9	George Williamson	Drummuie	"
774	"	6	4	Alex McIntosh	00	3	3	Alex McIntosh	Mosside	Rafford
775	"	"	"	Mary Robertson	00	12	17	Mrs Robertson	Bellevlair	none
776	"	"	"	Jeannie McIntosh	98	9	3	Alex McIntosh	Mosside	Rafford
777	"	"	"	John McIntosh	98	11	5	John McIntosh	Muir of Logie	Relugas
778	"	1	22	Alex McBain	94	11	6	Alex McBain	Lower Ardoch	Auldearn
779	"	5	14	John Dunbar	95	7	15	Wm Dunbar	Garvally	Relugas
780	"	6	4	Peter McIntosh	96	7	16	John McIntosh	Muir of Logie	"
781	"	"	"	Maggie McIntosh	94	7	10	"	"	"
782	"	"	11	Annie Shand	94	3	28	William Shand	Eireland	Lossiemouth
783	"	"	"	Bella Duncan	99	6	8	"	"	"
784	"	12	6	Robert Third	94	10	12	Robert Third	Cothall	Altyre
785	07	5	13	Jessie Hardie	01	10	8			"

Notes by Teacher and
Signatures of School Managers
with date of visit.

WHETHER EXEMPTION FROM RELIGIOUS INSTRUCTION IS CLAIMED	The highest standard in which he was there presented, and the results of his last EXAMINATION				Class into which admitted	Showing the Successive Standards in which presented in this School, with date and result of examination.						Showing the Specific Subjects in which he was presented in his LAST and in THIS School.																		EXACT DATE OF LEAVING			CAUSE OF LEAVING.
												STANDARD V		STANDARD VI		STANDARD Ex VI		STANDARD Ex Ex VI														
	Std	R	W	A		I	II	III	IV	V	VI	N° of Subject	Stage	N° of Subject	Stage	N° of Subject	Stage	N° of Subject	Stage	N° of Subject	Stage	N° of Subject	Stage	N° of Subject	Stage	N° of Subject	Stage	Year	Month	Day	

Successive Number (on admission or re-admission)	Date of Admission (on admission or re-admission)			Name in Full Christian and Surname	If Re-admitted Original Admission Number	Exact Date of Birth			Name and Address of Parent or Guardian		Last School Attended Before Entering This School
	Year	Month	Day			Year	Month	Day			
786	05	5	8	Mary Ann McIntosh		00	3	31	Wm McIntosh	Blackloch	
787	1907	9	18	Hester Thompson		01	11	3	James Thompson	Carnock	
788	"	"	23	Jeannie Logie		02	10	19	Wm Logie	Sluie Lodge	
789	"	"	"	Nellie Wilson		03	7	14	Geo Wilson	Eisland	
790	"	"	25	Mary A McGregor		02	12	4	McGregor	Ditch	
791	"			Alexr McIntosh					John McIntosh	Muir of Logie	
792	"	9	24	Willie McTavish		02	6	20	John McTavish	Carnock	
793	"	"	30	James Falconer		02	12	5	James Falconer	Drummuire	
794	"	10	21	Margaret Robertson		01	10	12	Robertson	Dunphail	
795	1908	1	21	William Boag		01	6	23	Mrs Boag	Longlea	
796	"	"	"	Eliz. A Boag		96	10	29	"	"	
797	07	6	3	Bella Wilson		95	10	13	George Wilson	Eisland	
798	1907	9	22	John A Davidson		99	5	16	Wm Davidson	Craigroy	
799	08	4	13	George Shipp		01	12	4	Garrow	Hillockhead	
800	"	"	"	Alexander Garrow		97	11	8	"	"	
801	"	10	12	Mary Dunbar		97	7	5	Wm Dunbar	Gervally	
802	"	3	31	Andrew Forbes		03	6	20	Andw Forbes	Ditch	
803	08	4	7	Willie Fraser		97	12	17	Fraser	Relugas	
804	"	10	12	Alexr Fraser		"			"	"	
805	"	6	15	Richard Stephen		98	8	23	C. Macrae	Drummuire	
806	"	10	7	George Forsyth		96	11	26	Forsyth	Relugas	
807	"	"	"	Frank Forsyth		01	10	31	"	"	
808	"			Alexr Fraser		03	7	24	Alexr Fraser	Dunphail Sq.	
809	"	6	15	Isabella Stephen		01	5	21	Alexr Stephen	Craighead	
810	"	10	9	Alexr McKenzie		99	6	16	Wm McHattie	Relugas	
811	09	4	11	Catherine Thompson		03	3	2	James Thompson	Carnock	none.
812	"	6	1	Thomas Clayton		99	6	23	Thomas Clayton	Relugas	Delnies
813	"	"	"	John Clayton		95	8	17	"	"	
814	"	"	8	Fergus G. Ferguson		01	6	8	Mrs Miller	Sluie Lodge	none
815	"	"	"	Jessie A. McKinnon		04	3	17	"	"	
816	"	7	5	Maggie Findlay		00	12	12	W McIntosh	Blackloch	
817	"	"	"	Annie Stephen		03	6	29	Alexr Stephen	Craighead	
818	"	"	19	George McGregor		04	12	29	Geo McGregor	Ditch	
819	"	9	21	George C Watt		97	11	17	John Watt	Relugas	
820	"	"	"	David Hardie		99	7	29	Wm Hardie	Altyre Cottages	
821	"	"	"	Bessie McKenzie					McKenzie		
822	"	"	"	Mary J McKenzie		98	1	11	"	"	
823	"	"	"	Maggie Hardie		97	7	21	Wm Hardie	"	
824	"	10	25	Lizzie Holmes		97	4	23	Mrs Holmes	Muir of Sluie	
825	"	11	1	Lydia McHattie		98	3	9	Alexr McHattie	Mosside	
826	"	"	"	Anabella McHattie		00	4	11	"	"	
827	"	1	29	Alexr Hardie					Wm Hardie	Altyre Cottages	
828	"	9	27	Jessie Dean					Mrs Hardie	Logie Farm	
829	"	"	10	James Thompson		04	10		James Thompson	Presly	
830	"	"	"	John Falconer		04	10	15	James F Falconer	Drumine	
831	"			Nettie Piercy		04	8	31	Adam Piercy	Sluie	
832	09	6	8	Jessie McKinnon		04	3	17	Mrs Miller	Do.	
833	10	6	6	Willie Robertson		04	7	26			
834	10	7	4	Michael Boag		04	7	4			
835	09	6	22	Willie McBain							

Notes by Teacher and Signatures of School Managers with date of visit.

WHETHER EXEMPTION FROM RELIGIOUS INSTRUCTION IS CLAIMED	The highest standard in which he was there presented, and the results of his last EXAMINATION				Class into which admitted	Showing the Successive Standards in which presented in this School, with date and result of examination.						Showing the Specific Subjects in which he was presented in his LAST and in THIS School.																			EXACT DATE OF LEAVING			CAUSE OF LEAVING.
	St⁴	R.	W.	A.		I	II	III	IV	V	VI	STANDARD V		STANDARD VI		STANDARD Ex VI		STANDARD Ex. Ex. VI											Year	Month	Day	
												N⁰ of Subject	Stage	N⁰ of Subject	Stage	N⁰ of Subject	Stage	N⁰ of Subject	Stage													

SUCCESSIVE NUMBER	DATE OF ADMISSION			NAME IN FULL	IF RE-ADMITTED ORIGINAL ADMISSION NUMBER	EXACT DATE OF BIRTH			NAME AND ADDRESS OF PARENT OR GUARDIAN		LAST SCHOOL ATTENDED BY ENTERING THIS SCHOOL
	Year	Month	Day	CHRISTIAN AND SURNAME		Year	Month	Day			
836	11	9	16	Margaret Wight		05	7	11	Wm Wight	Mosside	
837	"	4	27	Donald McBain		00	11	4	Alex McBain	Lower Ardoch	
838	10	"	22	Donald McTavish		05	7	8	John McTavish	Carnock	
839	26	11	26	George Jeans					Jas Jeans	Corsgrens	
831 8140	17	3	6	Nettie Piercy		04	8	31	Adam Piercy	Shire Mains	
8141	11	3	27	Alex Forbes		05	11	16	And Mr Forbes	Station Cottages	
842	11	4	17	James Cameron							
843	"	"	18	Alexander Cameron							
844	"	"	24	John Fraser		05	8	20	Jas Fraser	Moor of Shire	
845	11	5	31	Thomas McIntosh		00	6	17	— McIntosh	Blackloch	
846	"	"	"	Adam McIntosh		04 44	2 2	04 11	"	"	
847	"	"	"	Robina McIntosh		02	4	27	"	"	
848	"	6	2	David McIntosh		99	2	27	"	"	
849	"	"	5	Jessie A Fraser		04	9	23	Mrs Fraser	Clashdhu	
850	"	"	"	David Fraser		02	11	10	"	"	
851	"	"	"	Margaret Fraser		99	6	23	"	"	
852	"	"	7	Hugh Fraser		01	2	10	"	"	
853	"	7	6	Lilias McIntosh		06	6	4	McIntosh	Blackloch	
854	"	9	19	Charlotte McKenzie		01	3	8	Mrs McKenzie	Altyre	
855	"	"	"	Donald McLennan		"	6	11	— McLennan	Auldaushack	
856	"	"	28	Margaret May Watt		03	1	31	J. O. Watt	Relugas	
857	12	1	2	Jeannie Hardie		03	8	16	Wm Hardie	Altyre Cottages	
858	"	"	3	Florence McKenzie		"	1	31	Mrs McKenzie	Do Do	
859	"	"	11	George Grant		04	4	20	James Grant	Altyre Cottages	Altyre
860	11	12	4	Daisy Chisholm		00	10		— Chisholm	Bl Loch	
861	12	1	3	Peter Lander		00	8	31	Lander	Half Davoch	
862	"	"	27	Jean McIvor							
863	"	"	18	Jessie McIvor							
864	"	"	14	Helen Hardie		05	12	13	Wm Hardie	Altyre	
865	"	4	8	Donald Falconer		06	8	9	James Falconer	Drummine	
866	"	"	"	Ronald Hardie		07	6	1	Alex Hardie	Logie Mains	
867	"	"	9	Elsie McGregor		07	1	19	Geo McGregor	Ditch	
868	"	"	15	Caroline Thompson		07	3	3	James Thompson	Presly	
869	"	"	"	James Laing		04	6	9	Robert Laing	Auchmagarin	
870	"	"	"	Mary Laing		05	9	6	"	"	
871	"	6	4	Jessie McLeod		01	10	11	— McLeod	Downduff	
872	"	"	"	James McLeod		99 27	8 8	27 27	"	"	
873	"	"	5	Hugh McLeod		05	5	14	"	"	
874	"	"	6	Lizzie McLeod		03	9	7	"	"	
875	"	"	17	Nellie Cruickshank		02	11	2	— Cruickshank	Blackloch	
876	"	"	"	James Cruickshank		04	7	22	"	"	
877	"	"	"	Margaret McKay		00	7	9	Mrs Kennedy	Relugas	
878	"	"	26	Peter Cruickshank		06	12	22		Blackloch	
879	12	10	28	Donald McBain		00	11	4	Alex McBain	Lower Ardoch	
880				Hector Munro					Mrs Chisholm	Blackloch	
881				Donald Grant		07	2	9	James Grant	Altyre Cottages	None
882	13			Violet Thompson		08	2	23	James Thompson	Presly	
883	"			Mary J Simpson		01	4	23	William Simpson	Blackloch	Forres
884	"			George Simpson		04	8	12	Do	Do	Do
885	"			Katie Hardie		03	3	26	Mr Allan	Relugas	Shieldaig

Notes by Teacher and
Signatures of School Managers
with date of visit.

ETHER PTION FROM LIGIOUS UCTION CLAIMED	The highest standard in which he was there presented, and the results of his last EXAMINATION				Class into which admitted	Showing the Successive Standards in which presented in this School, with date and result of examination.						Showing the Specific Subjects in which he was presented in his LAST and in THIS School																EXACT DATE OF LEAVING			CAUSE OF LEAVING.
												STANDARD V		STANDARD VI		STANDARD Ex.VI		STANDARD Ex.Ex.VI											
	St⁴	R.	W.	A.		I	II.	III.	IV.	V	VI	Nº of Subject	Stage	Nº of Subject	Stage	Nº of Subject	Stage	Nº of Subject	Stage	Nº of Subject	Stage	Nº of Subject	Stage	Nº of Subject	Stage	Year	Month	Day	

Successive Number	Date of Admission (Year)	(Month)	(Day)	Name in Full (Christian and Surname)	Original Admission Number	Exact Date of Birth (Year)	(Month)	(Day)	Name of Parent or Guardian	Address	Last School Attended
886	13	4	7	Jessie Hardie		01	10	8	Mrs Allan	Relugas Village	Relugas
887	14	3	16	Nellie Anderson		04	4	9	William Anderson	Ditch	Dunphail
888	14	3	16	Robert Anderson		06	1	4	do	do	do
889	"	4	6	John Petrie		08	7	9	John Petrie	Ardoch Cottage	none
890	"	"	"	Ronald Rose		09	7	28	William Simpson	Blacklock	"
891	"	"	"	James McGregor		09	5	31	Geo McGregor	George McGregor Dure Lodge	"
892	"	"	"	Mary J. Falconer		08	7	16	James Falconer	Dreemine	"
893	"	"	29	Ella Laing		09	4	29	Robert Laing	Auchnagairn	"
894	"	5	4	Bella Hardie		08	8	26	William Hardie	Altyre Cottages	"
895	"	4	13	Frank Hardie		05	6	22	Mrs Allan	Relugas	Relugas
896	"	6	22	Jessie Robertson		03	3	18	James Robertson	Altyre	Rafford
897	"	"	"	Katie Robertson		05	1	5	"	Do	Do
898	15	1	6	George Rose		04	5	23	Hector Rose	Relugas	Relugas
899				Mary Strachan		07	12	4			
900	15	3	16	Robert Grant		09	2		James Grant	Altyre Cottage	none
901	15	4	12	Alexander Rose		06	1	15	Hector Rose	Relugas	Relugas
902	"	"	13	Harold J. Watt		05	12	13	John O. Watt	"	"
903	"	"	"	James A. Gordon		09	7	20	James Gordon	Longley Cottages	None
904	"	5	24	Clementina T. Grierson		04	6	9	Grierson	Chauffeur, Logie	Boxpole
905	15	4	26	Jessie A. Young		04	10	31	Miss Young	Moor of Sluie	Tore
906	"	"	"	Katie A. Young		07	1	2	"	"	"
907	"	"	"	Andrew Young		08	10	15	"	"	"
908	"	6	7	Bella M. Starkie		01	6	14	William Starkie	Church dhu	St Andrews Lhanbryde
909	"	"	"	Williamina Starkie		07	2	8	"	"	"
910	"	"	"	Ella Starkie		12	10	11	"	"	"
911	"	8	2	Annie Starkie		04	12	2	"	"	"
912	"	8	10	Jessie Dunbar		08	5	30	William Dunbar	Getrally	Dunphail
913	"	10	18	Betty Grierson		10	5	2	Grierson	Chauffeur, Logie	none
914	16	4	19	Jessie Hardie		12	1	16	Alex Hardie	Farmer Logie	"
915	"	"	"	Roderick J. McB Gordon		10	12	18	James Gordon	Longley Cottages	"
916	"	"	20	Chrissie Young		10	3	10	Miss Young	Moor of Sluie	"
917	"	"	24	Elizabeth Falconer		11	9	8	James Falconer	Dreemine	"
918	17	4	17	Chrissie Fraser		11	4	30	James Fraser	Moor of Sluie	"
919	"	"	"	Maggie Young		12	6	28	Miss Young	Do Do	"
920	"	5	16	Robert Forbes		14	4	20	Ant Forbes	Station Cottages Dunphail	
921	"	5	28	Evan Gordon		12	5	28	James Gordon	Lower Ardoch	
922 (890)	"	"	29	Ronald Rose or Simpson	890	09	7	28	W Simpson	Blacklock	Alves Public
923 (884)	"	"	"	Geo Simpson	884	04	8	12	Do	Do	Do
924	"	"	30	Jessie J. McIntyre		10	9	10	Mrs McIntyre	Woodhead	Grantown on Spey
925	"	"	"	Margaret E. McIntyre		08	12	11	Do	Do	Do
926	"	10	2	Cree Archibald		04	11	1	Mrs Cree	Eisland	Bentinck Sch Kilmarn
927	"	"	"	Cree Janet		08	11	11	" "	"	" "
928	"	"	5	Dey Christina B.		06	5	3	Mr Alex Dey	Altyre Cottages	Dava
929	"	"	"	Dey Louisa C.		09	6	13	Do Do	Do	Do
930	"	"	"	Dey John		11	11	17	"	"	Do
931	"	"	15	Cathie Christie					Mrs Tulloch	Moor of Sluie	Alves
932	18	3	18	George Calder		12	8	21	Professor Calder	Manchester University	none
933	"	4	9	Margaret Grierson		13	8	20			
934	"	"	10	Jean McGregor		13	5	16	George McGregor	Dure Lodge	none
935	"	6	4	Alex Prosser		05	10	10	Prosser	Lower Cothall	Kean

DATE OF ADMISSION 1913 TO 1918

...ether ...ion from ...igious ...uction ...laimed | The highest standard in which he was there presented, and the results of his last examination (Std., R., W., A.) | Class into which admitted | Showing the Successive Standards in which presented in this School, with date and result of examination (I., II., III., IV., V., VI.) | Showing the Specific Subjects in which he was presented in his LAST and in THIS School (Standard V, Standard VI, Standard Ex. VI, Standard Ex. Ex. VI — No. of Subject, Stage)

Exact Date of Leaving: Year	Month	Day	Cause of Leaving
			Schooling finished
			Do Do
			Do Do.
			Gone to Dunphail
26	5	22	" - Forres School
22	3	31	Gone to Forres School.
			Gone to Forres
			Exempted by E. A.
			Schooling finished
			Do Do
			Granted exemption
			Removed to Aberdeenshire
			Schooling finished
			Left district - gone to Lincoln[illegible]
			Schooling finished
			Left district
			Removed to Lincolnshire
			Dead.
			Schooling finished.
			Gone to Dunphail
			Gone to Forres.
			Left the District
			Gone to Rafford
			Gone to Forres
			Removed to Manchester.
			Gone to Grimsby
			Schooling finished
			Schooling finished

SUCCESSIVE NUMBER	DATE OF ADMISSION			NAME IN FULL	IF RE-ADMITTED ORIGINAL ADMISSION NUMBER	EXACT DATE OF BIRTH			NAME AND ADDRESS OF PARENT OR GUARDIAN		LAST SCHOOL ATTENDED BEFORE ENTERING THIS SCHOOL
	Year	Month	Day	CHRISTIAN AND SURNAME		Year	Month	Day			
936	18	6	4	William Prosser		07	5	15	Prosser	Lower Cothall	Keam
937	"	"	"	George Prosser		08	12	25	"	"	"
938	"	"	"	Elizabeth Prosser		10	12	3	"	"	"
939	18	5	6	Elizabeth Forrest		12	1		Mrs Anderson	Dluie Lodge	Ferness
940	18	7	30	Margaret Robertson		12	3	13	James Robertson	West Lodge Altyre	none
941	"	"	"	John Hardie		12	12	27	Wm Hardie	Cothall Cottages	"
942	18	8	6	Frank Calder					Professor Calder	Manchester University	"
943	"	10	14	Mary Strachan	899	07	12	4	Mrs Brown	Relugas Mains	Relugas
944	"	"	28	Alexander C. Garrow		08	1	15	Garrow	Cowgreens	Dyke
945	"	"	"	William Garrow		06	4	24	"	"	"
946	"	"	"	John James Garrow		10	1	26	"	"	"
947	"	"	"	Andrew Collie Garrow		12	10	26	"	"	"
948	19	1	13	James Hopkirk Simpson		06	3	8	James Simpson	Tilly Glens	Relugas
949	"	"	"	Alexander Simpson		07	8	28	"	"	Do.
950	19	4	21	William Falconer		13	10	8	James Falconer	Drumine	none
951	19	"	24	Helen M. Ross		12	1	19	Mrs Garrow	Carnock	Forres
952	"	"	"	Mary A. Garrow		13	12	19	Do	Do	none
953	"	5	5	Angus McPherson		14	9	14	Mrs McGregor	Dluie Lodge	"
954	"	"	"	Charles P. Williamson		10	10	6		Coxton	Forres
955	"	"	"	Mary Williamson		11	9	3		Do.	Do.
956	"	"	26	Jessie A. Cruickshank		14	1	31	Cruickshank	Drumine	none
957	"	6	24	Margaret A. Taylor		08	12	27	Taylor	Relugas Village	St Andrews Lhanbryd
958	"	"	3	John Blaikie		07	6	19	Walter Blaikie	Woodside Logie	Dunphail
959	19	"	"	Walter Blaikie		08	7	24	"	"	"
960	"	"	"	Margaret Blaikie		10	9	24	"	"	"
961	"	9	2	George Fraser					Fraser	North Lodge Dunphail	Forres
962	"	"	8	William Stronach		14			Stronach	Lodge Logie	none
963	19	12	5	Helen Prosser		13	5	28	Prosser	Cothall	"
964	20	2	16	Edith Blaikie		14	9	13	Walter Blaikie	Woodhead	none
965	20	4	13	John Elliott		10	3	8	William Elliott	Relugas	Muirdown Forgandenny
966	"	"	"	Margaret Elliott		12	12	16	"	"	do
967	"	"	"	Robina Elliott		14	10	14	"	"	do.
968	"	5	31	Peggie Reid		10	6	1	George Reid	Presley	Bergie
969	20	6	2	Roderick A. Macrae		14	11	15	Mrs Macrae	Dunphail	Dunphail
970	20	6	8	Isabella Reid					George Reid	Presley	Killas
971	20	6	28	Kenneth W. Harrower		10	2	22	Kenneth Harrower	Woodhead	Mordusk
972	"	"	"	Elsie M. Harrower		12	4	10	"	"	Mornish
973	"	"	"	Mary Isabel Harrower		13	3	29	"	"	"
974	"	9	27	Jeannie Cruickshank		08	1	2	Andrew Cruickshank	Down duff	Clatt
975	"	"	"	Agnes Cruickshank		11	3	22	Andrew Cruickshank	do.	Do.
976	"	"	21	Alexander Brander		15	9	9	Mrs Brander	School Cottage (P.O.)	Kingussie
977	"	11	2	William F. Fraser		07	4	4	John Garrow	Ardoch	Forres
978	21	4	12	Naomi Ivy Hardy		14	11	5	Wm Hardy	Cottages Altyre	none
979	"	"	"	Sara H. Fraser		15	10	26	Robert Fraser	Rose Cottage	"
980	"	"	"	Sheila C. Harrower		16	2	24	Kenneth Harrower	Woodhead	"
981	"	"	"	Isobel McRae		15	8	19	Mrs Macrae	Presley Cottage	"
982	"	"	13	Christina Garrow		14	10	24	John Garrow	Cothall	"
983	"	6	20	Agnes Jessie Dean					Mrs Dean	Logie Mains	
984	"	7	13	Willie Elliott		17	5	14	Wm Elliott	Relugas	"
985	"	6	6	Alexander Ross		10	10	6	Ross	Down duff Cottages	Auldearn

Notes by Teacher and
Signatures of School Managers
with date of visit.

WHETHER EXEMPTION FROM RELIGIOUS INSTRUCTION IS CLAIMED	The highest standard in which he was there presented and the results of his last EXAMINATION			Class into which admitted	Showing the Successive Standards in which presented in this School with date and result of examination.						Showing the Specific Subjects in which he was presented in his LAST and in THIS School.														EXACT DATE OF LEAVING			CAUSE OF LEAVING.
	St⁴	R.	W.	A.	I.	II.	III.	IV.	V.	VI	STANDARD V		STANDARD VI		STANDARD Ex VI		STANDARD Ex. Ex VI							Year	Month	Day	
																											Schooling over
																											Exempted by Authority
																											Gone to Forres
																											Age for leaving.
																											Removed to Manchester
																											Schooling finished
																											do do
																											Schooling finished
																											Schooling finished
																											Forres Academy.
																											Gone to Forres
																											do do
																											Removed to Daviot.
																											do Do
																											Forres Academy.
																											Gone to Relugas School.
																											Schooling finished
																											do do
																											Removed to Forres
																											Removed to Kinloss
																											Gone to Forres
																								21.	7	19	Left the District
																							"	"	"	do do
																							"	"	"	Do do
																										Gone to Rafford
																											Gone to Rafford
																											Removed to Rafford
																											Gone to Forres
																											" "
																											Schooling finished
																											Schooling finished.
																											Left for Canada
																											Schooling finished
																											Forres Academy
																											Forres Academy
																											Feb. School - Edenburgh
																											Left for London
																											Gone to Rothaugh Avoch

Successive Number	Date of Admission (Year/Month/Day)			Name in Full Christian and Surname	If Re-admitted Original Admission Number	Exact Date of Birth (Year/Month/Day)			Name and Address of Parent or Guardian		Last School Attended Before Entering This School
986	21	6	7	Hector Ogilvie		09	7	5	Mrs Ogilvie	Ramphlet Toll	Mosstowie
987	"	"	"	John Ogilvie		07	9	25	"	"	Do
988	"	4	12	Billy Calder		15	4	12	John Calder	Presley	none
989	"	9	"	James Cruickshank		16	6	20	James Cruickshank	Drummuir	"
990	"	"	"	Robert Anderson		17	2	8	James Anderson	Outlawell	
991	21	10	10	Ian Reid		09	10	14	William Reid	Dunphail Gardens	Dunphail
992	"	9	6	Lizzie Ogilvie		11	1	27	Mrs Ogilvie	Ramphlet Toll	Mosstowie
993	22	1	9	Margaret Taylor	957	08	12	27	Mrs Taylor	Relugas Village	Relugas
994	"	"	"	Andrew R. Taylor		12	10	22	"	"	Do.
995	"	"	"	Laurence Barnetson					William Barnetson	"	Do
996	"	"	"	John Callaghan					Mrs Clark	"	Do
997	"	"	"	Ruth McGregor		12	11	19	Peter McGregor	Culmony	Do
998	"	"		Willie Barnetson					Mrs Barnetson	Relugas Village	Do
999	"	"	30	John Barnetson		13	11	30	Do Do	Do Do	
1000	22	3	27	Thomas McIntosh		12	5	9	John McIntosh	Altyre Smithy	Forres
1001	"	"	"	Isa McIntosh		11	2	9	"	"	"
1002	"	"	"	Christina K. McIntosh		14	10	1	"	"	"
1003	"	"	"	Ella Calder		17	5	4	John Calder	Presley	none
1004	"	"	"	Annie McKenzie		16	8	14	James McKenzie	Araoch Cottage	"
1005	"	"	"	William McKenzie		18	3	7	"	"	"
1006	22	5	29	Hugh Cameron		5	5	7	Duncan Cameron	Logie Lodge	none
1007	"	"	30	Robert John McArthur		13	7	28	Robert McArthur	Muir of Logie	Kintessack
1008	"	"	"	William McArthur		14	11	16	"	"	"
1009	"	6	1	Ronaleyn Cameron		10	11	5	Duncan Cameron	Ploughman Presley	new Elgin
1010	"	"	"	Mary Bella Cameron		12	12	8	"	"	" "
1011	"	"	"	Daisy Cameron		13	12	8	"	"	" "
1012	"	"	"	Jessie Cameron		15	5	5	"	"	" "
1013	"	"	"	George Lyon Thom		11	7	24	William Thom	Ploughman Presley	Aberlour
1014	"	"	"	William Thom		09	12	28	"	"	Do.
1015	"	"	6	John Fraser		11	2	19	John Fraser	Ploughman Dounduff	East End Elgin
1016	"	"	"	William Fraser		13	4	23	"	"	"
1017	"	"	"	Donald Fraser		14	7	11	"	"	"
1018	"	"	7	Robert Fraser		08	8	28	"	"	"
1019	22	"	19	John McKenzie		15	7	18		Woodcutter Sluie	none
1020	"	11	23	Charlotte Henderson		16	4	8			"
1021	23	2	13	John Stewart		13	5	1	Donald	Dykeside	Forres Eppes
1022	"	"	"	Albert Stewart		15	4	27	"	"	"
1023	"	4	17	Kenneth Sinclair		11	2	24	Donald Sinclair	Dounduff	Dallas
1024	"	"	"	Donald Sinclair		12	11	25	"	"	do.
1025	23	5	31	Annie Young		10	11	1	William Young	Muir of Logie	Coneaveel
1026	23	9	4	Kelly McGregor		18	6	20	George McGregor	Dwie Lodge Logie	none
1027	"	"	"	Ella Shipp		17	12	23	George Shipp	Blairs In. Altyre	"
1028	"	"	"	Ian Calder		18	7	6	John Calder	Presley	"
1029	"	12	3	Roderick Gordon	915	10	12	18	James Gordon	Lower Diddch	Forres
1030	"	"	"	Evan Gordon	921	12	5	25	"	"	"
1031	"	12	10	William McCurrach		11	9	16	James May	Brachead	Gatmouth
1032	"	"	"	Walter McCurrach		14	1	31	"	"	Do.
1033	"	6	30	Reggie Stewart		17	9	27	Donald Stewart	Dykeside Rafford	none
1034	"	4	17	Frank Hardie		17	4	4	Wm Hardie	Altyre Cottages	None.
1035	"	"	"	Nellie Ogilvie		16	11	19	Mrs Ogilvie	Ramphlet Toll	"

Notes by Teacher and Signatures of School Managers with date of visit.

WHETHER EXEMPTION FROM RELIGIOUS INSTRUCTION IS CLAIMED	The highest standard in which he was there presented, and the results of his last EXAMINATION				Class into which admitted	Showing the Successive Standards in which presented in this School, with date and result of examination.						Showing the Specific Subjects in which he was presented in his LAST and in THIS School.																				EXACT DATE OF LEAVING			CAUSE OF LEAVING.
	Std	R.	W.	A.		I	II	III	IV	V	VI	STANDARD V		STANDARD VI		STANDARD Ex.VI		STANDARD Ex.Ex.VI												Year	Month	Day	
																																	Schooling finished
																																	Forres Academy
																																	" " "
																																	Forres Academy.
																																	Schooling over.
																																	Left for Canada
																																	Gone to live in Forres
																																	Removed to Nairn
																																	" "
																																	Schooling over
																																	Gone to Forres.
																																	" " "
																														24	5	27	Gone to Conicavel
																														24	5	27	Gone to Conicavel.
																														24	5	27	Gone to Conicavel
																																	Schooling finished.
																																	Forres Academy.
																														24	5	23	Gone to Nairn
																														24	5	2	Medically unfit
																														24	5	23	Gone to Nairn
																														24	5	12	Gone to Fortnightly School
																														24	5	16	" " "
																																	Forres Academy.
																																	Forres Academy.
																																	Forres Academy
																																	Schooling finished.
																														24	5	23	Gone to Nairn
																																	Gone to Forres Academy
																																	Schooling finished

Successive Number	Date of Admission or Re-Admission			Name in Full Christian and Surname	If Re-admitted Original Admission Number	Exact Date of Birth			Name and Address of Parent or Guardian		Last School Attended Before Entering This School
	Year	Month	Day			Year	Month	Day			
1036	24	4	22	Jessie Nicolson		14	11	12	John Nicolson	Relugas Mains	Relugas
1037	"	"	"	Edith Blaikie	963	14	9	13	Walter Blaikie	Woodhead	Forres Academy
1038	"	"	"	William Cruickshank		18	11	25	James Cruickshank	Drumine Cottage	None
1039	"	"	"	Duncan Cameron		19	11	9	Duncan Cameron	Logie	"
1040	"	"	"	James Henderson		18	12	14	Joseph Henderson	Sluie	"
1041	24	5	26	Alistair Macrae		18	8	13	Mrs. Macrae	Presley Cottage	"
1042	24	6	2	Jeannie Thomson		11	2	3	John Thomson	Blackloch	Rafford
1043	"	"	"	Charles Thomson		13	9	5	" "	"	"
1044	"	"	"	Annie Thomson		16	12	30	" "	"	"
1045	"	"	"	Violet Smith		15	4	7	Alexander Smith	Downduff	Forres Academy
1046	"	"	"	Daisy Smith		17	11	13	" "	"	"
1047	"	"	"	Margaret Macintosh		17	10	23	John Macintosh	Cothall, Altyre	None
1048	"	"	3	James Hutchison		13	9	5		Relugas Village	St. John's, Forres
1049	9	"	9	John Cruickshank		19	3	14	Mrs Cruickshank	The Ditch	None
1050	24	9	2	John Ross		20	11	13	John Ross	Coulmony	Dyke
1051	24	9	2	David Pirie		14	8	14	Wm Pirie	Coulmony	Dyke
1052	24	12	24	Alex Munro		14	7	14	Alex. Munro	Dykeside	Dyke
1053	25	2	9	Alistair Watt		14	10	23	Wm Watt	Relugas P.O.	Cawr
1054	25	2	9	Margaret Watt		16	5	9	" "	"	"
1055	25	4	21	Stuart Nicolson		16	10	4	John Nicolson	Relugas Mains	Relugas
1056	25	4	21	Caroline Hele Clark		20	2	3	Alexander Clark	Post Office, Logie	None
1057	25	4	21	Rosina Fraser		19	6	23	Robt. Fraser	Rose Cottage, Logie	None
1058	25	5	1	George Hutchison		13	8	19	John Hutchison	Blackloch	Rafford
1059	25	5	8	James Alexander Anderson		12	1	17	William Anderson	Half Davoch Cottages	St. John's, Forres
1060	25	5	8	Agnes Anderson		14	11	12	" "	"	"
1061	24	12	1	Mary Munro		16	10	9	Alex Munro	Dykeside	Dyke
1062	25	4	21	Charles Calder		20	7	12	John Calder	Presley Farm	None
1063	25	9	1	Alistair Turnbull Harrower		20	7	21	Kenneth Harrower	South Lodge, Logie	
1064	25	11	3	Jane Ann McLennan		20	4	10	John McLennan	Presley	Urquhart
1065	26	1	5	Margot Clark Brander		19	6	20	John Brander	Logie P.O.	Langdon, Alto Canal
1066	26	3	8	Nettie Hossack		16	11	20	Ebenezer Hossack	The Gardens, Relugas Ho.	Craigs P.S. Stirling
1067	26	4	21	Flora Munro		20	8	2	Alex Munro	Dykeside	None
1068	26	4	21	Wm Geo Shipps		20	8	2	Geo. Shipps	Cothall Altyre	None
1069	26	4	27	Edward Tough		20	1	5	John Tough	Cothall Altyre	None
1070	26	4	27	Anna Tough		21	2	12	John Tough	Cothall Altyre	None
1071	26	7	28	Ina Dey		15	7	28	James Dey	Presley Cottage	Forres Academy
1072	26	8	26	Annie Ogilvie		20	7	27	Mrs Ogilvie	Ranph let J.M.	None
1073	26	8	30	Robt Tomis Anderson		20	9	3	William Anderson	Half Davoch Cottage	None
1074	27	4	19	Elsie Coutts Nicolson		17	4	1	John Nicolson	Relugas Mains	Relugas
1075	27	4	19	Susanna McIntosh		21	12	9	John McIntosh	Cothall Altyre	None
1076	27	4	19	Janet Shipps		11	9	8	George Shipp	Aidoch, Dunphail	" "
1077	27	4	19	Jas Falconer Anderson		21	1	12	James Anderson	Outlawell	" "
1078	27	4	19	Douglas McKenzie		2	1	11	James McKenzie	Logie Lodge	" "
1079	27	4	19	Wm Falconer		2	1	11	Jas Falconer	Rose Villa, Blairs, Forres	" "
1080	27	4	19	Alex John Noble Walton		3	3	22	James Walton	Aitside	" "
1081	27	5	2	Vernon Strafford		20	5	16	Thos. W. Strafford	The Aidoch	Westness land, School Newcastle
1082	27	6	2	George Hutchison	1058	13	8	19	John Hutchison	Blackloch	Kinloss
1083	27	6	6	Harvey G. McPherson		13	8	13	Alex. McPherson	Presley	None
1084	27	8	30	Adam Strathdee		16	11	2	Adam Strathdee	Cowgreens	Half Davoch
1085	27	8	30	Helen W. Turnbull		19	2	13	John Turnbull	Estate, Logie	Fraserburgh

Notes by Teacher and
Signatures of School Managers
with date of visit.

WHETHER EXEMPTION FROM RELIGIOUS INSTRUCTION IS CLAIMED	The highest standard in which he was there presented, and the results of his last EXAMINATION				Class into which admitted	Showing the Successive Standards in which presented in this School, with date and result of examination.						Showing the Specific Subjects in which he was presented in his LAST and in THIS School																EXACT DATE OF LEAVING			CAUSE OF LEAVING.
	St⁴	R	W	A		I	II	III	IV	V	VI	STANDARD V		STANDARD VI		STANDARD Ex.VI		STANDARD Ex. Ex.VI									Year	Month	Day	
																														Forres Academy.
																														Age for leaving
																														Forres Academy.
																														Forres Academy
																														Th Academy Edinburgh
																														Schooling finished
																														Left the district
																														" " "
																														Nairn
																														Schooling Finished
																														Forres
																														Gone to Rafford
																														Schooling finished
																														Gone to Aberdeen
																														" " "
																														Schooling Finished
																														Forres Academy.
																														Schooling finished
																														Gone to Kilross
																														Schooling finished
																														Schooling finished
																														Gone to Forres.
																														Forres Academy
																														Forres Academy
																														Forres Academy
																														Left the district
																														Forres Academy.
																														Left the district
																														Forres Academy
																														Forres Academy
																														Gone to Forres.
																														Relugas School
																														Schooling Finished
																														Forres Academy
																														Left District
																														Left the district.
																														Forres Academy
																														Left the district
																														Forres Academy.
																														Left the district
																														Gone to Forres. Left Sch
																														Left District
																														Schooling Finished
																										24	9	30	Gone to Aberdeen.

SUCCESSIVE NUMBER (ON ADMISSION OR RE-ADMISSION)	DATE OF ADMISSION OR RE-ADMISSION			NAME IN FULL CHRISTIAN AND SURNAME	IF RE-ADMITTED ORIGINAL ADMISSION NUMBER	EXACT DATE OF BIRTH			NAME AND ADDRESS OF PARENT OR GUARDIAN		LAST SCHOOL ATTENDED BEFORE ENTERING THIS SCHOOL
	Year	Month	Day			Year	Month	Day			
1086	27	9	27	Margaret Grant		3		5	Woodhead Cottage	James Grant	Elgin West End
1087	27	9	5	James A Grant					" "	" "	" "
1088	27	9	5	Edith Grant		22	1		" "	" "	" "
1089	28	4	17	John Anderson					Oakwell	James Anderson	None
1090	28	4	17	Helen F. Falconer					Blairs Farm	James Falconer	None
1091	28	4	17	Ian M Harrower					South Lodge	Kenneth	None
1092	28	6	4	Elizabeth Anderson		1			Relugas	John	Dyke
1093	27	8	28	Pat Wayfas J. McIntyre					Buckie P.S.	James	Woodhead
1094	"	"	"	Gladys M. McIntyre					Buckie P.S.	James	"
1095	"	"	"	Norman R. McIntyre		10	11	74	Buckie P.S.	James	"
1096	"	"	"	John Alexander McIntyre		3	1	13	Buckie P.S.	James	"
1097	"	"	"	Alethia R. MacD McPherson		23			Presley	Alexander	None
1098	"	"	"	John G. Grant		3			Woodhead	James	None
1099	"	"	"	Jack M. Nicholson		8	8	5	Relugas Mains	John	Relugas
1100	"	"	"	George McB Calder		5	11	7	Presley	John	None
1101	"	"	"	Margaret Walker		71	1	16	Cowgreens, Dunphail	M.A. Strathdee	None
1102	28	12	3	James McPherson		1	1		Mill of Logie	James McPherson	Crucivel
1103	28	12	3	Walter McPherson		17	1	1	" "	" "	"
1104	29	1	15	George Milne		1	11		Relugas	Andrew	Ferness
1105	29	4	29	Mary Helen Tough		7		3	Cothall, Altyre	John	None
1106	29	4	29	Margaret Maclennan		17	17	7	Presley Cottage	John	"
1107	29	4	29	Kathleen Piercy Steward		13	7		Logie Home Farm	James	"
1108	29	4	29	Jean Melvin Clark		3	3		Logie Post Office		"
1109	29	4	29	Amelia Murray Watson		5	3	20	Hillside	James	"
1110	29	6	5	Margaret Ogilvie		26	3		Ramphlit Toll	Mrs McDonald	"
1111	29	8	27	Simon Morrison McLennan		111			Auchnagairn	Donald	Glen Ferness
1112	29	8	24	James Alex Shipp		211		1	Ardoch, Dunphail	George	None
1113	29	8	28	Munro, Frank J.		28			Blair's Cottage	Robert	"
1114	29	8	28	Kenneth Chisholm		28			Sluie Lodge	Thomas	"
1115	29	8	28	William Chisholm		211			Sluie Lodge	Thomas	"
1116	29	9	3	Isaac W. Paterson		1			Presley	Alex	"
1117	29	9	3	Jemima U. Paterson		21			Presley	Alex	"
1118	30	1	6	David Grant McKenzie		2	12	12	Cowgreens		None
1119	30	4	21	Jean Winifred Anderson		2			Oakwell	James	"
1120	30	4	21	Elsie May		7	4	6	Hall Wood Cottages	James	"
1121	30	4	28	Thelma Wight			12		Moss Side	Mrs W. Wight	"
1122	30	6	2	Edward James Taylor		25			Blairs Farm, Altyre	Edward	"
1123	30	6	2	Alexander Falconer		26	8		" "	Alexander	"
1124	30	6	2	Mary Jane Grant		21	8	8	" "	William	"
1125	30	6	3	Mary McCaig		7	7	2	" "	John	Drainie
1126	30	6	3	John McCaig		26	10	1	" "	"	"
1127	30	9	1	William John Fraser McDonald		26			Ardoch, Dunphail	William	None
1128	31	2	3	Margaret Matilda Keiro		2	11		Altyre	Stephen	Alves
1129	31	4	13	Barbara Grant		23			Woodhead	James	None
1130	31	4	13	Alan Logan Harrower					South Lodge	Kenneth	"
1131	31	4	13	George Alexander Taylor		29	2	21	Altyre	Edward	Dyke
1132	31	4	13	George Taylor Hay		29	1	2	Altyre	James	"
1133	31	4	13	Audrey Allan Hay		26	11	21	Altyre	James	"
1134	31	4	13	Ella Amelia Murray Bisset		26	1	13	Blackloch	William Arthur	"
1135	31	4	13	Isabella Maclennan		26	10	7	Presley Cottages	John	"

Notes by Teacher and Signatures of School Managers with date of visit.

1105 First entry made by me on appointment as Headmaster. James B Pratt

WHETHER EXEMPTION FROM RELIGIOUS INSTRUCTION IS CLAIMED	The highest standard in which he was there presented, and the results of his last EXAMINATION				Class into which admitted	Showing the Successive Standards in which presented in this School, with date and result of examination.						Showing the Specific Subjects in which he was presented in his LAST and in THIS School.																EXACT DATE OF LEAVING			CAUSE OF LEAVING.
	St.d	R.	W.	A.		I.	II.	III.	IV.	V.	VI.	STANDARD V		STANDARD VI		STANDARD Ex.VI		STANDARD Ex.Ex.VI								Year	Month	Day	
																													Forres Academy.
																													"
																													Forres Academy
																													Forres Academy.
																													Forres Academy.
																													Schooling Finished
																													Forres Academy.
																													Forres Academy.
																													" "
																													" "
																													Left District
																													Forres Academy
																													Schooling Finished.
																													Forres Academy.
																													Forres Academy.
																													Left District
																													Left District
																													Left District
																													Gone to Forres.
																													Forres Academy.
																										32	5	24	Left District
																													Forres Academy.
																													Schooling Finished.
																													Schooling Finished
																													Left District
																										29	9	2	Left District Gone to Conicavel.
																													Left District
																													" "
																													" "
																													" "
																													Schooling Finished
																													Forres Academy.
																													Forres Academy.
																													Forres Academy
																										32	5	24	Left District
																										33	5	19	Left District Gone to Half Davoch.
																													Left District
																													"
																													"
																													Left District
																													Returned to Alves
																													Left District Forres Academy
																													"
																													Forres Academy
																										32	5	24	Left District
																													Forres Academy
																													"
																													"
																													"

Successive Number	Date of Admission or Re-Admission Year	Month	Day	Name in Full Christian and Surname	If Re-admitted Original Admission Number	Exact Date of Birth Year	Month	Day	Name and Address of Parent or Guardian		Last School Attended Before Entering This School
1136	31	5	5	James Wright Stewart			8	8	James	Home Farm, Logie	none
1137	31	6	1	Roy Anderson			3		John	Blairs Farm, Altyre	Betty West
1138	31	6	1	John Singer Anderson			8		"	" "	Petty West
1139	31	6	1	James Gordon Smith			14		James	Blairs Farm Altyre	Drainie
1140	31	6	1	William John Smith			5		"	" "	none
1141	31	6	4	Annie Mackay			3		Donald	Downduff	Moyness
1142	31	6	4	Donald Mackay					"	"	"
1143	31	9	1	Mary Christina Falconer					Alexander	Blairs Farm Altyre	none
1144	31	9	1	Edyth Mary Paterson Fraser					James	Cothall Altyre	none
1145	31	9	1	James Fraser					James	Relugas Cottage	Relugas
1146	31	9	1	Jane Elizabeth Ogilvie		6	6	23	Mrs McDonald	Ramphlet Toll	none
1147	31	10	26	Kenneth Chisholm	1114		6	23	Thomas Anderson	Presley	Loch Laggan
1148	31	10	26	William C Chisholm	1115		4		"	Presley	Loch Laggan
1149	31	11	2	Thomas Anderson					Thomas	Presley	none
1150	31	11	2	Jean Ann Anderson			8		"	Presley	none
1151	31	12	7	Catherine McDonald					James	Ardoch Cottage	Conicavel
1152	31	12	7	Isabella McDonald					"	"	"
1153	31	12	7	James Ramsay McDonald					"	"	"
1154	31	12	7	William George McDonald					"	"	"
1155	32	4	5	Jessie Anderson					James	Outlawell	none
1156	32	4	5	Catherine Elizabeth Watson					James	Hillside	"
1157	32	4	6	Robert Strachan					Mary Strachan	Ardoch	"
1158	32	4	11	Alex. Nicolson					John	Relugas Mains	"
1159	32	5	30	John McBain					William	Muir Cottage	Forres
1160	32	5	30	Alex. McBain					"	"	"
1161	32	5	30	Elizabeth McBain					"	"	"
1162	32	6	6	Catherine McDonald					William	Blairs Farm Altyre	Ferness
1163	32	6	20	George M Grant					Charles	"	Drainie
1164	32	8	30	Richard Smith					Thomas	North Lodge Logie	none
1165	32	8	30	Laura A K Fraser					James	Cothall Altyre	none
1166	33	1	9	Marion Eliza McIntosh					George	Cothall Altyre	none
1167	33	4	18	John Robertson					J. J. Robertson	Blackloch	none
1168	33	4	18	George Andrew McKenzie					William	The Neuk Logie	none
1169	33	6	5	Charles Reid					James	Cothall Altyre	Oldmeldrum
1170	33	6	5	John Reid					"	"	"
1171	33	8	29	Ida May					James	Woodview Cottages	none
1172	33	10	11	Edyth M P Fraser	1144				James	West Lodge Altyre	Turriff
1173	33	10	11	Laura A K Fraser	1165				"	"	"
1174	33	10	30	George Andrew McKenzie	1168				William	Ardoch Cottage	Half Davoch
1175	34	4	9	Isabel Mary Falconer					James	Drumine	none
1178	34	8	28	John Campbell					John	The Ditch Logie	none
1179	34	8	28	Robert John Anderson					Thomas	Presley	"
1180	34	8	28	Janet McDonald					Robert	Ramphlet Toll	"
1181	34	8	28	Margaret McCabe					Peter	Logie	Auchterarder
1182	34	8	29	Duncan Clark					Donald	Blackloch	Relugas
1183	34	8	29	Elizabeth Clark					"	"	"
1184	34	8	29	James Clark					"	"	"
1185	34	8	29	Margaret Clark					"	"	"
1186	34	8	29	John Clark					"	"	"

Notes by Teacher and
Signatures of School Managers
with date of visit.

WHETHER EXEMPTION FROM RELIGIOUS INSTRUCTION IS CLAIMED	The highest standard in which he was there presented, and the results of his last EXAMINATION				Class into which admitted	Showing the Successive Standards in which presented in this School, with date and result of examination.						Showing the Specific Subjects in which he was presented in his LAST and in THIS School.																		EXACT DATE OF LEAVING			CAUSE OF LEAVING.
	St⁴	R.	W.	A.		I	II	III.	IV.	V	VI	STANDARD V		STANDARD VI		STANDARD Ex.VI.		STANDARD Ex.Ex.VI.									Year	Month	Day	
																											32	5	2 Y	Left District.
																											32	5	2 Y	"
																											32	5	2 Y	"
																											32	5	2 Y	"
																											32	5	2 Y	"
																											23	12	32	Schooling Finished
																														Transferred to Relugas School
																											53	5	19	Left District gone to Half Davoch
																														Forres Academy
																														Transferred to Relugas School
																														Forres Academy.
																														Schooling Finished.
																														Schooling Finished.
																														Schooling Finished
																											32	5	2 Y	Left District.
																											32	5	2 Y	"
																											32	5	2 Y	"
																											32	5	2 Y	"
																														Forres Academy
																														" "
																														Left District for Relugas
																														Transferred to Relugas
																														Schooling Finished
																											34	6	7	Schooling Finished.
																														Schooling Finished
																														Schooling Finished.
																														Forres Academy
																														"
																														"
																														Left District.
																														Left District.
																														Schooling Finished
																														Forres Academy
																														" "
																														Forres Academy
																														"
																														Left District.
																														Forres Academy.
																														Schooling Finished
																														Schooling Finished
																														Forres Academy
																														Forres Academy.
																														Forres Academy
																														Schooling Finished
																														Forres Academy.
																														Schooling Finished
																														Forres Academy.

SUCCESSIVE NUMBER (ON ADMISSION OR RE-ADMISSION)	DATE OF ADMISSION OR RE-ADMISSION			NAME IN FULL CHRISTIAN AND SURNAME	IF RE-ADMITTED ORIGINAL ADMISSION NUMBER	EXACT DATE OF BIRTH			NAME AND ADDRESS OF PARENT OR GUARDIAN		LAST SCHOOL ATTENDED BEFORE ENTERING THIS SCHOOL
	Year	Month	Day			Year	Month	Day			
1187	34	9	3	Alexander Falconer	1123	20			Alexander	Cowgreens	Half-Davoch
1188	34	9	3	Mary Falconer	1143	23		25	"	"	Half-Davoch
1189	34	9	3	Jeannie Falconer		26		2	"	"	"
1190	35	4	16	Margaret Lawrence		22		21	Robert	Blairs Cottages	None.
1191	35	4	15	Alastair Anderson		22	12	P.	James	Cutlawell	"
1192	35	4	15	Forbes McKenzie		24		21	William	Ardoch Cottage	"
1193	35	4	15	Mona Helen Bisset		29		22	Arthur	Brachead	"
1194	35	8	28	Mary Elizabeth Mathison		21		21	Mrs Strathdee	Hillockhead	"
1195	35	10	2	Gertrude Joyce Robertson		21			Mother.	Presley Cottage	Conicavel.
1196	36	1	6	Jean Melvin Clark	1108	2		3	Mother	Post Office Logie	
1197	36	4	14	John Alex. McDonald		28		5	Father.	Ramphlet Cottage	None.
1198	36	4	14	Ada Falconer		38		8	"	Drumine	"
1199	36	4	14	William McKenzie.		6		1	"	Ardoch Cottage	"
1200	36	4	14	Luke Grant		2		7	"	Blairs Altyre	"
1201	36	4	14	Eliz. Ella. Anderson		2			"	Presley Cottages	"
1202	36	4	14	Eliz. McKenzie Smith		21	2	211	"	North Lodge Logie	"
1203	36	4	14	Mary H. Smith		3		23	"	North Lodge Logie	"
1204	36	4	14	Iris Audrey Harper		3		3.	"	Peathillock	"
1205	36	6	1	William McLennan		3		9	"	Blairs, Altyre	Inchberry.
1206	36	6	1	Helen McLennan		12			"	"	"
1207	36	8	31	George McGregor Shaw					Mr McGregor	West Lodge	Dundee
1208	36	8	31	Jessie Shaw					"	"	
1209	37	4	6	Peter McCabe		2			Father	Greenkeeper's Cottage	None.
1210	37	4	6	George Macaulay Pratt		31		21	"	Schoolhouse Logie	"
1216	37	4	6	Margaret Campbell		32	2	P.	"	The Ditch	"
1212	37	4	6	Beryl Doreen Harper		3			"	Peathillock	"
1218	37	4	6	Ina McCallum Smith		5			"	North Lodge	"
1214	37	5	31	John Robert Harrold		5			"	Home Farm, Logie	Relugas
1215	37	5	31	George McIntosh		23	30		"	Clashdhu	Kellas
1216	37	5	31	James McIntosh		33	3	31	"	Clashdhu	Kellas
1217	37	6	14	Margaret Hay		23			"	Moss Side	Relugas
1218	37	6	17	Alexander Hay		6			"	Moss Side	Relugas
1219	37	6	17	James Hay		6			"	Moss Side	Relugas
1220	37	11	3	Catherine E. McKenzie		2			"	Blairs Farm Altyre	Kintessack.
1221	38	1	14	Robert Campbell		1			"	Peat Hillock	Relugas
1222	38	4	12	Alexander Grant		2		1	Mr McKenzie	Woodview Cottages	None
1223	38	4	12	Kenneth McLennan		2		1	Father	Presley Cottages	"
1224	38	4	13	George Hector McDonald		22		22	"	Ramphlett Toll	"
1225	38	4	18	Isabella Jane Grant		2	2	1	"	Blairs Farm Altyre	"
1226	38	5	30	Margaret E. Green		2			"	Logie Home Farm	Aberlour.
1227	38	6	6	Margaret Steele		21		11	"	Ardoch Cottage	Forres
1228	39	4	11	Gordon Dick		5		41	"	Cothall Cottages	None.
1229	39	4	11	Janet Campbell		3		2	"	The Ditch	"
1230	39	4	11	Edward Jas. Grant		22		3	"	Blairs Farm	"
1231	39	4	11	Alistair May		6		5	"	Woodview Cottages	"
1232	39	4	11	William McKenzie McBain		34		41	"	Muir of Logie	"
1233	39	4	11	James Randall Pratt		34	4	41	"	Schoolhouse	"
1234	37	8	26	Margaret Dick		24		8	"	Cothall Altyre	"
1235	39	5	30	Elsie Milton		21	1	7	"	Blairs Farm Altyre	West End Elgin
1236	39	5	30	Helen Milton		23	1	7	"	"	"

Notes by Teacher and
Signatures of School Managers
with date of visit.

WHETHER EXEMPTION FROM RELIGIOUS INSTRUCTION IS CLAIMED	The highest standard in which he was there presented and the results of his last EXAMINATION				Class into which admitted	Showing the Successive Standards in which presented in this School, with date and result of examination.						Showing the Specific Subjects in which he was presented in his LAST and in THIS School.														EXACT DATE OF LEAVING			CAUSE OF LEAVING.
	St⁴	R.	W.	A		I	II	III	IV	V	VI	STANDARD V		STANDARD VI		STANDARD Ex.VI		STANDARD Ex.Ex.VI						Year	Month	Day	
												Nᵒ of Subject	Stage	Nᵒ of Subject	Stage	Nᵒ of Subject	Stage	Nᵒ of Subject	Stage								
																											Schooling Finished
																											Forres Academy.
																											" "
																											Left "District".
																											Relugas School
																											Left District
																											Left District.
																											Left District.
																							36	5	22	Left District.
																											Forres Academy.
																											Forres Academy.
																											" "
																											Left District
																											Gone to Burgie
																											Forres Academy.
																											Left for Medical Reasons.
																											Forres Academy
																											Left District.
																											Schooling Finished.
																							39	5	26	Left District.
																											Left District.
																											Left District.
																											Forres Academy.
																											Forres Academy.
																											Gone to Dunphail
																											Left District
																											Forres Academy
																											Gone to Glenerness
																											Gone to Dallas
																											" " "
																											Forres Academy
																											Schooling Finished
																											Forres Academy.
																											Forres
																											Schooling Finished
																											Forres Academy
																											Forres Academy
																											Forres Academy
																											Left District
																											Forres Academy
																							39	5	26	Left District.
																											Left District
																											Left District.
																											Left District.
																											Left Schooling Finished
																											Left District.
																											Forres Academy.
																											Forres Academy.
																											Schooling Finished
																											Forres Academy

Successive Number	Date of Admission Year	Month	Day	Name in Full Christian and Surname	If Re-admitted Original Admission Number	Exact Date of Birth Year	Month	Day	Name and Address of Parent or Guardian		Last School Attended Before Entering This School
1234	39	5	30	Marjorie Milton					Father	Blairs Farm Altyre	West End Elgin
1238	39	5	31	Dorothy Henderson		8			James	Blairs Farm Altyre	Marybank Ross-sh
1239	39	6	5	Robert McDonald		8	6	0	James	Logie Toll	Glenferness
1240	39	6	5	Jane M. McDonald		0	6	8	"	"	"
1241	39	6	5	Mary Ann McDonald		6	6	5	"	"	"
1242	39	6	5	Adam Strathdee					Robert	Hillockhead	Rafford
1243	39	6	5	Donald Garrow					Father	Ardoch Cottage	Nethy Bridge
1244	39	6	5	James Garrow					"	"	Nethy Bridge
1245	39	6	5	Margaret A. Garrow		8	6		"	"	"
1246	39	9	7	Margaret C. Mackay		5	5	3	c/o McCabe	Grankeeper's Cottage	Myopia School
1247	39	9	7	George Walker					c/o McKenzie	Cothall Altyre	Granton, Edin
1248	39	9	7	William Park		3			c/o McCallum	Cothall Altyre	" "
1249	39	9	12	Alister Yaneton		6		6	c/o McDonald	Logie Toll	North Berwick
1250	39	9	19	Stewart Davidson				6	% Hen Anderson	The Stables, Altyre	Northfleet Kent
1251	39	8	24	Mary A. Strathdee		5	7		Father	Hillockhead	None
1252	39	8	24	William Fettes		5	0		Father	Doonduff	Relugas
1253	39	11	13	Isabella McK. Simpson		4			c/o McKenzie	Altyre	Edinburgh
1254	40	2	5	Sinclair Nicholson					James	Coston Sawmills	Douglas, Lanark
1255	40	2	5	Elizabeth Nicholson		3	3		"	"	"
1256	40	4	4	James Wm Falconer					James	Drumine	None
1257	40	4	4	Robert Garrow						Ardoch Cottage	"
1258	40	4	4	Allan R.S. Harper				3	Henry	Divie Lodge	"
1259	40	4	4	Hugh McCallum Smith					Tom	North Lodge	"
1260	40	4	4	Margaret Strathdee				3	Robert	Cothall Altyre	"
1261	40	4	4	Gordon Fraser					Mr Fraser	Rose Cottage	"
1262	40	4	22	Wm Taylor Cruickshank					Mr Taylor	Coston Sawmills	Aboyne
1263	40	5	22	Henry Lorimer			2		William	"	Dallas
1264	40	5	22	Fred Alex Lorimer					"		
1265	40	5	29	Janet Fettes		23	3	3	William	Braehead	Relugas
1266	40	6	3	Elizabeth H. Fettes		8	6	04	William	"	
1267	40	8	29	Sheila E.H. Lindsay		3			Andrew	Presley Cottage	Colinton, Edinburgh
1268	40	9	2	Mary Robban			1	1	Mrs Murdoch	Blairs, Altyre	None
1269	40	11	4	Dagne Day			1	1	Charles	Woodhead	Stockbridge, Edin
1270	41	3	3	Walter Cumming					Walter	Altyre	Dunphail
1271	41	4	22	Dagne Day	1269				Charles	Woodhead	Stockbridge Edin
1272	41	4	22	Rosemary F. McKenzie			9		Colin	Altyre	None
1273	41	4	22	Catherine A. Nicholson				1	James	Coston Sawmill	"
1274	41	4	22	Annabelle C. Piercy		32			John	Sluie	"
1275	41	4	22	Sophie D.W. McArthur				1	David	Clashdhu	"
1276	41	4	22	James Green		31			James	Home Farm Logie	"
1277	41	4	22	Ewen J. Macarthur				5	Hugh	Longley	"
1278	41	4	22	Robert McDonald				2	Robert	Ramphlet Toll	"
1279	41	5	19	Ronald Taylor					Mr Anderson	The Stables Altyre	Hayfield St. Glasgow
1280	41	5	26	Peter J.S. Philips		10	1		William	Coston Sawmills Altyre	Kinneivie Banff
1281	41	5	26	Annie J.W. Philips		33	3		William	Coston Sawmills, Altyre	"
1282	41	6	24	Helen Jean Andrew					George	Altyre	Drainie
1283	41	6	9	Helen Rose Clark			1		George	Blairs Farm	Forgandenny
1284	41	6	9	Alistair Clark					"	"	"
1285	41	6	9	John Sinclair Clark		6			"	"	"
1286	41	6	9	Stanley Clark		23	1	13	"	"	"

Notes by Teacher and
Signatures of School Managers
with date of visit.

WHETHER EXEMPTION FROM RELIGIOUS INSTRUCTION IS CLAIMED	The highest standard in which he was there presented, and the results of his last EXAMINATION				Class into which admitted	Showing the Successive Standards in which presented in this School, with date and result of examination.						Showing the Specific Subjects in which he was presented in his LAST and in THIS School.																		EXACT DATE OF LEAVING			CAUSE OF LEAVING.
	St⁴	R	W	A		I	II	III	IV	V	VI	STANDARD V			STANDARD VI			STANDARD Ex VI			STANDARD Ex Ex VI							Year	Month	Day	
												Nᵒ of Subject	Stage		Nᵒ of Subject	Stage		Nᵒ of Subject	Stage		Nᵒ of Subject	Stage									
																															Forres Academy
																															Schooling Finished.
																															Granted Exemption.
																												5	7	43	Left District
																												5	7	43	Left District.
																															Left District
																															Left District
																															"
																															"
																															Returned to Edinburgh
																															Returned to Granton.
																															" " "
																															Left District.
																															Returned to Kent
																															Left District.
																															Schooling Finished
																															Returned to Edinburgh
																															Left District
																															Left District.
																															Forres Academy.
																															Left District.
																															Left District.
																															Forres Academy.
																															Left District.
																															Forres Academy
																															Schooling Finished.
																															Left District.
																															Left District.
																															Forres Academy
																															Left District.
																															Gone to Dallas
																															Left District.
																															Returned to Edinburgh.
																															Left District
																															Returned to Edinburgh
																															Gone to Forres
																															Left District
																															Forres Academy.
																															Left District.
																															Left District
																															Left District.
																															Forres Academy
																															Returned to Glasgow.
																															Left District
																															Left District
																															Forres Academy
																															Left District
																															Left District.
																															Left District
																															Left District

SUCCESSIVE NUMBER (ON ADMISSION OR RE-ADMISSION)	DATE OF ADMISSION (OR RE-ADMISSION) Year	Month	Day	NAME IN FULL CHRISTIAN AND SURNAME	IF RE-ADMITTED ORIGINAL ADMISSION NUMBER	EXACT DATE OF BIRTH Year	Month	Day	NAME AND ADDRESS OF PARENT OR GUARDIAN		LAST SCHOOL ATTENDED BEFORE ENTERING THIS SCHOOL
1284	41	6	9	Elizabeth Mary Clark		34	4	18	George	Blair Farm	Forgandenny
1288	41	6	9	Archibald Clark		3		3	"	"	"
1289	41	6	9	William A. Morrison		5			William	Coston Sawmills	Pluscarden
1290	41	6	9	Manuel J. Morrison		3			"	"	"
1291	41	6	9	Catherine A. "		3			"	"	"
1292	41	6	9	Ronald Clark		3		5	George	Blair Farm	Forgandenny
1293	41	8	12	Edwin Donald Souter		3	1	0	Mrs Souter	Cothall, Altyre	None
1294	41	10	24	Mary Shand		3			c/o Fettes	Braehead	Fochabers
~~1295~~	~~42~~	~~2~~	~~16~~	~~Margaret McKenzie~~		3		5	John	Sluie Croft	Laurencekirk
1295	41	11	17	James Allan		3			Hugh Campbell	Peathillock	Auldearn
1296	41	11	17	Elizabeth Allan		3		15	"	"	Auldearn
1297	42	2	16	Margaret McKenzie		3		5	John	Sluie Croft	Laurencekirk
1298	42	4	14	Angus M. Pratt		35			James	Schoolhouse	None
1299	42	4	14	Mary Anderson		31			James	Cutlawell	"
1300	42	4	14	Patricia Falconer		31		4	James	Drumine	"
1301	42	4	14	Elsie McDonald		31	5	2	James	Logie Toll	"
1302	42	4	14	Sandra M. Piercy		1	5		John	Mains of Sluie	"
1303	42	5	6	Heather Black		38		2	David	Muir Logie	Relugas
1304	42	6	1	James Murdoch		3	6		James	Clashdhu	Forres
1305	42	9	15	Elizabeth Denoon		34	4	13		Coston	
1306	42	10	5	Andrew Nicholson		31	2	13	James	Altyre	None
1307	42	11	23	Alistair Ganson					Mrs McDonald	Logie Toll	
1308	42	12	21	William Stables		34		3	William	Coston	
1309	43	4	24	John McDonald		3			James	Logie Toll	None
1310	43	4	24	Dorcas K.C. Gillanders		3			John	Braehead	Relugas
1311	43	4	24	Williamina D. Philips		3		23	William	Coston	None
1312	43	4	24	Lorna Stables		3			William	Coston	None
1313	43	5	4	Helen E. Nicholson		3			James	Altyre	None
1314	43	5	5	June M. Ross		34			Mrs McDonald	Ramphlett	"
1315	43	5	10	Alan Gillanders		33		23	John	Braehead	None
1316	43	5	31	James Ross		30	10	11	Mrs Ross	Home Farm Logie	Pluscarden
1317	43	6	7	James Cameron		31			Richard	The Ditch	Llanbryde
1318	43	8	3	Richard Cameron		32		14	"	"	Llanbryde
1319	43	8	3	James G. Rae		33	9	1	William	Longley Cottage	Newtonmore
1320	43	8	3	Barbara G. Rae		3		5	"	"	"
1321	43	8	25	Margaret McDonald	1240				James		
1322	43	8	25	Mary McDonald	1241				"		
1323	43	8	25	Elsie McDonald	1301				"		
1324	43	8	25	John McDonald	1309				"		
1325	43	8	30	Alistair Ganson	1249						
1326	43	9	6	Annie Angus		3			Mrs Gillanders	Braehead	
1327	43	11	1	Ewen J. MacArthur	1247				Hugh	Muir of Logie	Killin
1328	43	11	1	Ann MacArthur		34	4		"	"	"
1329	44	2	14	Alistair Ganson	1249						
1330	44	3	20	Alistair Ganson	1249						
1331	44	4	18	Mary Milton		40			Alexander	Blairs Altyre	None
1332	44	4	18	M. Ann Smith		40	4	4	Tom	North Lodge	None
1333	44	4	18	Francis McD Philips		38	10	14	William	Coston	None
1334	44	4	24	Ian G. Bridgeford		38	22		John	Home Farm Logie	Scatwell (Ros)
1335	44	4	24	Edward M. Bridgeford		3		11	"	" " "	Scatwell (Ross)

Notes by Teacher and Signatures of School Managers with date of visit.

WHETHER EXEMPTION FROM RELIGIOUS INSTRUCTION IS CLAIMED	The highest standard in which he was there presented and the results of his last EXAMINATION				Class into which admitted	Showing the Successive Standards in which presented in this School, with date and result of examination.						Showing the Specific Subjects in which he was presented in his LAST and in THIS School.																		EXACT DATE OF LEAVING			CAUSE OF LEAVING.
	St⁴	R.	W.	A.		I	II	III	IV	V	VI	STANDARD V		STANDARD VI		STANDARD Ex VI		STANDARD Ex. Ex VI										Year	Month	Day	
																															Left District
																															" "
																															Gone to Dunphail
																															"
																															Left District
																												49	8	23	Forres Academy.
																															Returned to Fochabers
																															Schooling Finished
																															Forres Academy.
																															Left District.
																												49	8	23	Forres Academy.
																												49	8	23	Forres Academy.
																												49	8	23	Forres Academy
																															Left District.
																												49	8	23	Forres Academy.
																															Returned to Refugees
		,	.	.																											Forres Academy.
																															Left District
						.بال١١																										Left District
																															Left District.
																															Left District
																															Left District.
																															Left District.
																															Left District.
																															Left District.
																															Left District.
																															Left District
									.																						Schooling Finished
																															Forres Academy
																															Forres Academy.
																															Gone to Dunphail
																															Gone to Dunphail
																															Left District
																															"
																															"
																															"
																															Left District.
																															Left District
																															"
																															"
																															"
																															Left District
																															Forres Academy.
																															Left District
																															Forres Academy.
																															Forres Academy

SUCCESSIVE NUMBER	DATE OF ADMISSION			NAME IN FULL CHRISTIAN AND SURNAME	IF RE-ADMITTED ORIGINAL ADMISSION NUMBER	EXACT DATE OF BIRTH			NAME AND ADDRESS OF PARENT OR GUARDIAN		LAST SCHOOL ATTENDED BEFORE ENTERING THIS SCHOOL
	Year	Month	Day			Year	Month	Day			
1336	44	4	24	Margaret A. Bridgeford					John	Home Farm Logie	Scatwell, Ross-shire
1337	44	5	29	Ethel L. MacKay				5	Mother	Blair's Farm	Spynie
1338	44	5	29	Helen Leggat						"	"
1339	44	8	1	Ann Callow					Father	Cothall	London
1340	44	8	1	John Ross Morrison					John	Coston	Forres
1341	44	10	30	Helen M. Riach		14	11	13	Alex.	Dounie Sawmill	Auldearn
1342	45	1	3	Wm Gordon Strachan					Donald	Coston	
1343	45	4	10	Christina Wright					Gordon	County Cottages	None
1344	45	4	10	David H. Wright					"	"	"
1345	45	4	10	Margaret Gardiner			12	10	Richard	Blair's Farm	"
1346	45	4	10	Christina Nicholson					Cothall James	Cothall	"
1347	45	4	10	Elspeth A. Strachan					Donald	Coston	"
1348	45	4	10	James Riach Keith					Lewis	Divie Lodge	"
1349	45	4	10	William Hay					William	Logie Home Farm	"
1350	45	4	10	James E. Souter						Gregory	"
1351	45	4	10	James A. Riach			31	13	Alex.	Dounie Sawmill	"
1352	45	4	10	Alan Dick					William	Cothall Cottages	"
1353	45	4	10	George Stables					William	Coston	"
1354	45	4	10	George Macrae MacDonald	56				Peter	Coston	"
1355	45	4	10	David Bryan Thomson					James	Mains of Logie	"
1356	45	5	21	Christina Eliz. Grant					Father	Dunphail	Elgin
1357	45	5	22	Fred. George Walker	45				George	Old Blairs Altyre	None
1358	45	10	16	William John W. Riddell	42				Mrs M. Riddell	Coston	Rothiemay
1359	45	11	26	Robert Rhind				3	Mrs Harrold	Dounie Sawmill	Dunphail
1360	45	12	3	Alex. Cowie Morrison				10	Mrs McLennan	Coston	Bogmuchalls
1361	46	3	12	Jessie Lillie Robertson			2		William	Head Keeper's Cottage Altyre	Banavie
1362	46	3	12	Allan Wm Kennedy Robertson			8	2	"	"	"
1363	46	3	12	Robert Robertson			2		"	"	"
1364	46	4	16	Thomas Bell Smith					Thomas	North Lodge Logie	None
1365	46	4	16	Betty McKenzie		12	3		Robert	Cothall, Altyre	Half Davoch
1366	46	4	16	George McKenzie					Robert	"	"
1367	46	4	16	Joyce McKenzie		5	3	3	William	Cullawell Cottage	Rafford
1368	46	4	16	Robert McKenzie					"	"	"
1369	46	4	16	Christina McKenzie				3	"	"	"
1370	46	4	17	Jennifer Jackson		10	14		Mrs Jackson	The Cottage, Presley	Edinburgh
1371	46	4	22	Robin de J. Jackson					"	"	Edinburgh Academy
1372	46	4	22	Alexander McKenzie		4			William	Cullawell Cottage	None
1373	46	4	23	Duncan Sharp		11			Mr Ettles	Coston	Portsoy
1374	46	5	20	Robert Andrew Beattie						Blairs Farm	Alves
1375	46	6	10	Sheila Stewart Singer						"	Rafford
1376	46	8	13	Malcolm MacMartin Reid					Walter	Pealhillock	Dunphail
1377	46	8	13	Hamish Peter Reid			5	5	"	"	"
1378	46	8	13	Clementine Eliz. Reid		5	3		"	"	"
1379	46	8	13	Donald Cameron Reid		3		4	"	"	"
1380	46	8	13	Iain Padruig Reid		10		3	"	"	"
1381	46	8	13	Garrick William Strain		4	8	8		Cothall, Altyre	
1382	46	8	13	Isobel Grant Morrison			8	8		Woodhead Logie	None
1383	46	8	13	Sheena Mary Beattie		11	2	25		Blairs Farm Altyre	None
1384	46	8	13	Alistair Grant McDonald			12	2	Robert	Ramphlet Toll	None
1385	47	4	28	Thomas Dean Spence		16			James	The Neuk	Rothes

Notes by Teacher and
Signatures of School Managers
with date of visit.

WHETHER EXEMPTION FROM RELIGIOUS INSTRUCTION IS CLAIMED	The highest standard in which he was there presented and the results of his last EXAMINATION				Class into which admitted	Showing the Successive Standards in which presented in this School, with date and result of examination.						Showing the Specific Subjects in which he was presented in his LAST and in THIS School.																EXACT DATE OF LEAVING			CAUSE OF LEAVING.
	Std	R	W	A		I	II	III	IV	V	VI	STANDARD V		STANDARD VI		STANDARD Ex.VI		STANDARD Ex.Ex.VI								Year	Month	Day	

Cause of Leaving entries:

- Forres Academy.
- Left District
- " "
- Forres Academy.
- Gone to Inverness-shire
- Left District.
- Forres Academy
- "
- Killed in Accident at her home.
- Left District.
- "
- Forres Academy.
- Left District.
- Forres Academy
- Gone to Inverness-shire.
- Left District
- " "
- " "
- " "
- Schooling Finished
- Gone to Rafford.
- Left District.
- Left District.
- "
- Forres Academy
- "
- "
- Forres Academy.
- Gone to Relugas
- Forres Academy.
- "
- "
- Returned to Edinburgh
- "
- Forres Academy [53 8 19]
- Left District
- Left District.
- Left District
- Schooling Finished
- Left District
- "
- "
- "
- Gone to Glass Huntly
- Forres Academy
- Left District
- Forres Academy.
- Gone to Park Nairn

Successive Number	Date of Admission			Name in Full (Christian and Surname)	If Re-admitted Original Admission Number	Exact Date of Birth			Name and Address of Parent or Guardian		Last School Attended Before Entering This School
	Year	Month	Day			Year	Month	Day			
1386	47	4	28	Barbara Mary Spence			2	12	James	The Neuk	Rothes
1387	47	5	26	Marjory Jarron			3	11	William	Blairs Farm	Dyke
1388	47	5	26	Ronald Jarron			11		William	Blairs Farm	Dyke
1389	47	8	12	Alan Dick	1352		11		William	Cothall Cottages	Golspie
1390	47	8	12	Robert Colin Cameron		2	10	16	Richard	The Ditch	None
1391	47	10	13	Donald P. Falconer			5	13	Donald	Cutlawell	Returned to England
1392	47	10	24	Jane Patricia Falconer		13	13	1	"	"	"
1393	48	1	19	Peter Rennie Wilson			1	1	William	Blairs Farm	Aberlour
1394	48	1	19	Magdalene Mary Wilson			2	12	"	"	"
1395	48	1	19	Roger Allan Wilson			10	20	"	"	"
1396	48	4	13	Patricia Eliz. Wright		18	15	10	Gordon	County Cottages	None
1397	48	4	13	Eileen Milton		48		5	Alexander	Blairs Farm	"
1398	48	4	13	Sheena W.D. Anderson		42	12	22		"	
1399	48	4	13	Ada Doris Wilson		48	2	2	William	"	None
1400	48	8	24	Jim McKenzie		48	13	10	William	Cutlawell	None
1401	48	8	24	Annie G. D. Anderson		3	3	16	Mrs Anderson	Blairs Farm	None
1402	48	8	30	Alistair Wm Thom		43		7	Alexander	Divie Lodge	None
1403	49	4	19	William Garden						Sluie Crofts	Dunphail
1404	49	4	19	James Garden		2		5		"	"
1405	49	4	19	William Alex. Chalmers		4		8		Logie Toll	None
1406	49	4	19	James Moir Calder		44		8	John	Presley	"
1407	49	4	19	John Lewis Leith		43	2	7	Mrs Leith	North Lodge	"
1408	49	4	19	Heather Ann Clark		43	12	22	Arthur	Gamekeepers Cottage	"
1409	49	5	3	Lydia Finnie					James	Blairs Farm	Rafford
1410	49	5	3	George M. Finnie		2		2	"	"	"
1411	49	5	3	Alex. Benzie Finnie		41	4	14	"	"	"
1412	49	5	9	Sheila Hendry		41				Blairs Farm	
1413	49	5	9	Muriel Hendry		48	10	20		"	
1414	49	5	23	Barbara Jane Jeffrey Finnie		44		1	James	Blairs Farm	None
1415	49	8	23	Elizabeth Grant		43	10	1	Richard	Relugas Mains Cott	Relugas
1416	49	8	23	Hugh Grant		41		2	"	"	"
1417	49	8	23	George Milne						Doonduff Cottages	"
1418	49	8	23	Violet Milne		40		11		"	"
1419	49	8	23	Christopher K. Milne		43				"	"
1420	49	8	23	Douglas S. Milne		44	5	5		"	"
1421	49	8	23	Alexander Raeburn						"	"
1423	49	8	23	Mabel Clark		40	5	11	David	Doonduff Lodge	"
1424	49	8	23	Marjorie J Clark		43	11	1	"	"	"
1425	49	8	23	Rosabel Stuart		40			William	Doonduff	"
1426	49	8	23	Margaret Stuart		41	1	7	"	"	"
1427	49	8	23	William J Jamieson		44	2		William	Relugas	"
1428	49	8	23	William Morrison		44	4	7		Relugas	"
1429	49	8	23	George McCurrach						County Cottages	
1430	49	8	23	James Simpson		43	11	1	James	Tillyglens	"
1431	49	8	24	Sheena J. A. Mackie		41			Miss McPherson	Blairs Farm	Wales
1432	49	8	24	Jessie Duncan		49	5	50	John	"	
1433	49	8	24	Ian Duncan		43	4	4	"	"	
1434	49	12	12	John Grubb		44	12	1			
1435	50	4	18	Walter J. Jamieson		47	4	18	William	Relugas	None
1436	50	4	18	John L. Stewart		43	11	10	William	Doonduff	None

Notes by Teacher and
Signatures of School Managers
with date of visit.

WHETHER EXEMPTION FROM RELIGIOUS INSTRUCTION IS CLAIMED	The highest standard in which he was there presented, and the results of his last EXAMINATION				Class into which admitted	Showing the Successive Standards in which presented in this School, with date and result of examination.						Showing the Specific Subjects in which he was presented in his LAST and in THIS School.																		EXACT DATE OF LEAVING			CAUSE OF LEAVING.
	Std	R.	W.	A.		I	II	III	IV	V	VI	STANDARD V		STANDARD VI		STANDARD Ex. VI		STANDARD Ex. Ex. VI								Year	Month	Day	
												Nº of Subject	Stage	Nº of Subject	Stage	Nº of Subject	Stage	Nº of Subject	Stage										
																										48	4	2	Left District.
																										47	10	31	Left District
																										47	10	31	" "
																													Forres Academy.
																										54	8	23	Forres Academy.
																										48	3	5	Returned to England
																										48	3	5	"
																										48	8	24	Forres Academy.
																													Left District.
																													Killed in Road Accident.
																										52	12	1	Gone to Delnies.
																													Gone to Mundole, Forres.
																													Left District.
																													Left District.
																										53	6	30	Left District Forres Academy
																													Left District.
																										52	2	14	Gone to Ellon, Aberdeenshire
																													Gone to Rafford.
																													"
																													To Urquhart.
																										56	8	21	Forres Academy
																										53	8	14	Forres Academy
																													To Carron.
																													Left District
																													"
																										49	8	23	Left District.
																													"
																										49	8	23	Left District.
																													"
																													Forres Academy.
																										53	3	9	Gone to Conicavel.
																													Left District
																													"
																													"
																													"
																													"
																													Forres Academy.
																										55	6	30	"
																										53	8	19	Nairn Academy
																										54	8	23	" "
																										56	8	21	Forres Academy
																										56	8	21	To Suez Canal Zone
																													Forres Academy
																										52	5	30	Gone to Hatton, Aberdeenshire
																													Left District
																													"
																													"
																										54	8	20	Forres Academy
																										54	8	20	Forres Academy

Successive Number	Date of Admission or Re-admission			Name in Full (Christian and Surname)	If Re-admitted Original Admission Number	Exact Date of Birth			Name and Address of Parent or Guardian		Last School Attended Before Entering This School
	Year	Month	Day			Year	Month	Day			
1434	50	4	18	William J. Young			11		John	Jillyglens	None
1448	50	4	18	Helen P. M. Grant		4	4	1	Richard	Relugas Mains	"
1449	50	4	18	Kathleen Henry		4				Blairs Farm Altyre	"
1450	50	4	18	Caroline M. Raffel		4			James	Logie Post Office	"
1451	50	4	18	Irene C. Thom		45	18	19	Alexander	Durie Lodge	"
1452	50	9	13	Marion E. Porter		42	10	18	William	Blairs Farm Altyre	Alford Aberdeenshire
1453	50	9	13	William A. Porter		40	10	5	"	"	"
1454	50	9	19	William J. McBey		40		3	William	Blairs Farm "	Alves
1455	50	9	19	Malcolm A. Georgie		43	13	2	"	"	"
1456	50	10	30	William Davidson		42	2		Gordon	"	"
1457	50	11	7	Edith Will		41	11	2	Alex	Ardoch	Fettercairn
1458	50	11	7	Doreen Will		42	1		"	"	"
1459	50	11	7	Ann Will		44	1		"	"	"
1460	51	2	6	Allan W. Wood		44	9		Leslie	Blairs Farm Altyre	Ellon
1461	51	2	12	Alastair M. Bowie		49	9		Miss J. Bowie	Doonduff Cottages	Dallas
1462	51	4	17	Gordon F. Cameron					Richard	The Ditch	None
1463	51	4	17	Ian MacKenzie		46	1		William	Cuthawell Cottage	"
1464	51	4	17	Sheila MacDonald		45	11	24	Robert	Ramphlet Toll	"
1465	51	4	17	Sheila Morrison					Alex	Relugas	"
1466	46	7	16	Gladys M. Porter		46	1	2	William	Blairs Farm Altyre	"
1467	51	4	23	Colin J. Appleyard		42			Ronald	Muir of Sluie	Yorkshire
1468	51	4	23	Lorna E. Appleyard		44	6		"		"
1469	51	8	21	Marie Warden		44	6		James	The Kennels Coulmony	Ninsihant
1469	51	8	21	John Grant		45	3	13	John	Blairs Farm Altyre	Balogie
1470	51	8	21	Christina Stuart		43	3	31	William	Doonduff	None
1471	51	8	21	Doris Wood		41			Leslie	Blairs Farm Altyre	"
1472	52	4	15	Barbara Dick		46	1	4	William	Cothall Altyre	"
1473	52	4	15	Angela J. G. Rule or May		40	4	3	Mrs Rule	Relugas Mill	"
1474	52	4	15	Joyce Warden		41			James	The Kennels Coulmony	"
1475	52	4	15	Wallis McDonald		21			Charles	Home Farm Logie	"
1476	52	4	15	Alisdair Urquhart		46			William	The Garage, Logie	"
1477	52	4	24	Re Caroline M. Raffel	1450	46			James	P.O. Logie	Kinloss
1478	52	6	3	James Wishart Robinson		45	10	3	Ian	Home Farm Logie	Dunphail
1479	52	8	19	Margaret Ann Mitchell		46	6	3		Blairs, Altyre	
1480	52	8	19	Sheila Barbara Manson Grant		47	3	1	George	Wardend, Altyre	None
1481	52	8	19	Marion Mitchell Wood		47	8		Leslie	Blairs Altyre	None
1482	52	8	19	Grace Gordon Wright		48	4	8	Gordon	County Cottages	None
1483	52	9	16	Margarette Ann Watson		46	4	13	Henry	Blairs, Altyre	Enzie
1484	52	9	16	Henry William Watson		46	4	28	"	"	"
1485	52	10	29	Phyllis Fettes		42	10		George	Doonduff Cottages	Kinloss
1486	52	10	29	Elizabeth Fettes		43	10	13	"	"	"
1487	52	10	29	Moira Fettes		45	11		"	"	"
1488	42	10	30	James Fettes		47	11	9	"	"	"
1489	53	1	26	Mary Ashcroft			2	2	Mrs Grant	Wardend, Altyre	Keith
1490	53	3	10	May Janina Forbes		43	4	23	Charles	Home Farm Logie	Burghead
1491	53	3	30	Evelyn Mary Grant		46	4		Edward	West Lodge Dunphail	Rothes
1492	53	4	15	Marjory Elizabeth Robinson		48	4	11	Ian Clark	Home Farm Logie	None
1493	53	4	15	Hazel Isabel McBean		48	1	6	Hugh	The Kennels, Relugas	"
1494	53	4	15	Aden A. Bisset Grant			3	9	Donald	Relugas P.O.	"
1495	53	4	15	Patricia Ann Bruce		46	2	11	William	Blairs Farm Altyre	"

Notes by Teacher and Signatures of School Managers with date of visit

WHETHER EXEMPTION FROM RELIGIOUS INSTRUCTION IS CLAIMED	The highest standard in which he was there presented, and the results of his last EXAMINATION				Class into which admitted	Showing the Successive Standards in which presented in this School, with date and result of examination.						Showing the Specific Subjects in which he was presented in his LAST and in THIS School.																	EXACT DATE OF LEAVING			CAUSE OF LEAVING.
	Std	R	W	A		I	II	III	IV	V	VI	STANDARD V			STANDARD VI			STANDARD Ex.VI			STANDARD			Ex.Ex.VI			Year	Month	Day	
																												52	4	15	Gone to Dunphail District
																												53	3	9	Gone to Conicavel
																															Left District
																															To R.A.F. Kinloss.
																												52	2	14	Gone to Ellon Aberdeenshire
																															Left District
																															"
																															Forres Academy.
																															Left District.
																															"
																															Forres Academy.
																															Gone to Angus.
																															"
																												53	8	19	Forres Academy
																												55	6	30	"
																															Left District
																												58	8	19	Forres Academy.
																												54	8	20	Dunphail.
																												58	8	19	Forres Academy.
																															Left District
																															Gone to Balloch, Inverness.
																															"
																															Nairn Academy.
																												54	5	13	Gone to Rayne, Aberdeenshire
																												58	8	19	Forres Academy.
																												54	5	13	Gone to Gartly, Aberdeenshire
																												59	6	26	Forres Academy.
																															Left District
																												59	6	26	Nairn Academy.
																															To Dallas.
																												59	6	26	Forres Academy Kinloss.
																												52	5	21	Returned to Kinloss
																												59	8	30	Forres Academy.
																												52	8	28	Kintessack
																												53	8	28	To Kintessach
																															To Perthshire.
																												54	5	13	Gone to Gartly Aberdeenshire
																												52	12	1	Gone to Delnies
																															To Alves.
																															To Fornighty
																															"
																															"
																															Nairn Academy.
																															Forres Academy.
																												53	10	16	Gone to Alves
																															To Dunphail
																												60	7	1	Forres Academy
																												60	7	1	" "
																												60	7	1	" "
																															To Kintessack

SUCCESSIVE NUMBER (ON ADMISSION OR RE-ADMISSION)	DATE OF ADMISSION OR RE-ADMISSION			NAME IN FULL CHRISTIAN AND SURNAME	IF RE-ADMITTED ORIGINAL ADMISSION NUMBER	EXACT DATE OF I.TH.			NAME AND ADDRESS OF PARENT OR GUARDIAN		LAST SCHOOL ATTENDED BEFORE ENTERING THIS SCHOOL
	Year	Month	Day			Year	Month	Day			
1496	50 47	4 10	15 14	Eleanor Jean Stuart		10	0	14	William	Doonduff	None.
1497	53	4	15	Jean Ann Morrison		3	9	8	Alex.	Relugas	"
1498	53	4	15	June Fettes		3	3		George	Doonduff Cottage	"
1499	53	5	6	Caroline Raffel					James	Post Office, Logie	Kinloss.
1500	53	5	27	William James Stephen		11	1	3	William	Blairs, Altyre	
1501	53	6	8	Shirley Hadden			1		"	Post Office, Logie	Kennethmont
1502	53	6	8	Margaret Hadden		4	7		"		
1503	53	8	19	Leslie Barbour Stephen		3			"	Blairs, Altyre	none
1504	53	8	19	Alan MacKenzie		3	4		"	Outlawell	"
1506	53	8	19	Rosemary Murray		6			George	Ardoch	Aboyne
1507	53	8	19	George Murray		7	9	2	"	"	"
1508	53	11	2	Daisy Ross		21	13		James	Home Farm, Logie	Aldourie Inverness
1509	54	2	8	Agnes Marion Burnett		7	1	7	Mr. Clark	Muir of Logie	
1510	54	3	8	Robert Lappin Pozzi		5	12			Greenkeeper's Cottage, Logie	
1511	54	3	16	Patricia Cran			4	6		Coulmony.	Abriachan Inverness
1512	54	4	20	Angela Rule		45	5	23	Mrs Rule	Doonduff Cottages	Cannich.
1513	54	4	20	Andrew Jas. May Rule		17	1		"	"	None.
1514	54	4	20	George David Urquhart		4	1	3	William	The Garage, Logie	None.
1515	54	5	14	Ada Doris Wilson	1399	4	3		William	Blairs Farm, Altyre	Kinloss
1516	54	8	23	Agnes Allison		4	9		Mrs Grant	Wardend, Altyre	Kennoway, Fife
1617	54	8	23	Margaret Ingram		45		7	Father	Doonduff Cottages	England.
1518	54	8	23	William McLean		45		3	John	South Lodge, Altyre	None
1519	54	9	21	Isobel Gordon		47	8	2		Blairs Farm, Altyre	Balnacoul
1520	54	10	4	William James Gordon		45	2		"		"
1521	54	8	23	Charles Simpson		44	6	10	Mrs Campbell	Peathillock, Logie	Rafford
1522	54	10	19	David Innes Cameron		45	11	1	John	Blairs Farm	Kinloss
1523	54	10	19	Sheila Ann Cameron		47	1		"	" "	"
1524	55	4	13	Dora Orr Campbell		5	1		Robert	Peathillock, Logie	None
1525	55	4	13	John Alex. Grant					Donald	Relugas	None
1526	55	8	23	James Castles		4			James	Blairs Farm, Altyre	Rosisle
1527	55	8	23	Irene Castles		43	1		"	"	"
1528	55	8	23	Dennis Castles		46	10	3	"	"	"
1529	55	8	23	Edna Castles		ED M			"	"	"
1530	55	8	23	Wm. L. Morris		ED	5		Laurence	Lower Cothall	Barthol Chapel
1531	55	8	23	Elizabeth Morris		ED		7	"	"	"
1532	55	9	12	Marion Burnett	1509	47			Mr Clark	The Muir	
1533	55	9	12	Irene Burnett		49			"	"	
1534	55	10	26	Isobel Mary Michie						Blairs Farm, Altyre	Rhynie Aberdeenshire
1535	55	10	25	Francis Michie		47				"	"
1536	55	10	25	Margaret Michie		4	6			"	"
1537	55	11	28	Roderick D. Lawson		42	2	4		West Lodge, Relugas	Forres Primary
1538	56	1	5	Gwendoline Geddie		5				Blairs Farm, Altyre	Mosstowie
1539	56	1	9	Caroline Raffel	1450	44	1	5	James	Post Office, Logie	Mingoay, Cornwall
1540	56	1	16	Brian Peach		4	5	3		Blairs Farm, Altyre	Portsoy
1541	56	1	16	Stanley Peach		4				"	"
1542	56	1	30	Margaret Peach		1				" " "	"
1543	56	4	11	Thomas Alex Taylor		4	6	6	Thomas	Coston	Auldearn
1544	56	4	11	Alexander F. Taylor		4			"	"	"
1545	56	1	23	Nellie Jean Geddie		6	5	5		Blairs Farm, Altyre	Mosstowie
1546	56	4	11	Dennis Fraser		50	4	12		" " "	None.

Notes by Teacher and Signatures of School Managers with date of visit.

WHETHER EXEMPTION FROM RELIGIOUS INSTRUCTION IS CLAIMED	The highest standard in which he was there presented, and the results of his last EXAMINATION				Class into which admitted	Showing the Successive Standards in which presented in this School, with date and result of examination.						Showing the Specific Subjects, in which he was presented in his LAST and in THIS School.										EXACT DATE OF LEAVING			CAUSE OF LEAVING.
	Stᵈ	R.	W.	A.		I	II	III	IV	V	VI	STANDARD V	STANDARD VI	STANDARD Ex VI	STANDARD Ex. Ex. VI						Year	Month	Day	
																					60	7	1	Forres Academy
																					60	7	1	" "
																								Left District.
																								Returned to Kinloss
																					53	11	24	To Newburgh Aberdeenshire.
																								Returned to Kennethmont
																					53	11	24	To Newburgh Aberdeenshire
																					62	7	7	Forres Academy
																					60	7	1	Forres Academy
																					58	8	19	Forres Academy.
																					59	6	26	Forres Academy
																					54	8	23	Forres. Academy.
																								Returned to Edzell
																					56	10	16	Gone to Orton
																								Left District
																								Gone to Whitebridge.
																								"
																					61	7	1	Forres Academy
																					55	8	30	Secondary up to
																					56	2	13	Gone to Kinloss.
																					55	6	30	Left District.
																					59	5	26	Gone to Aberdeenshire
																					62	7	12	Forres Academy
																					56	10	8	Gone to Ellon Aberdeenshire
																					56	10	8	"
																					56	10	8	"
																					56	10	8	"
																								To Huntly.
																					60	7	1	Forres Academy
																					55	11	10	Returned to Edzell.
																					55	11	10	"
																					54	8	20	Forres Academy.
																					60	7	1	Forres Academy
																					61	7	1	Forres Academy
																					60	7	1	Forres Academy
																					61	7	1	" "
																					56	4	24	Gone to Germany
																					56	10	29	Gone to Inverness-
																					56	10	29	"
																					56	10	29	"
																					59	1	5	Gone to Forres
																					59	1	5	"
																					62	7	5	Forres Academy
																					59	10	2	Removed to Forres

Successive Number (on admission or re-admission)	Date of Admission or Re-admission Year	Month	Day	Name in Full Christian and Surname	If Re-admitted Original Admission Number	Exact Date of Birth Year	Month	Day	Name and Address of Parent or Guardian		Last School Attended before Entering this School
1547	56	4	11	Janet Dorothea Marshall						Stables, Altyre.	None.
1548	56	4	11	Marjorie Lynne Raffle						Post Office, Logie	"
1549	56	4	30	Shirley Ann Hadden					Mrs Hadden	" " "	Kinsthmont
1550	56	4	30	Margaret Hadden					"	"	"
1551	56	4	30	Hector Hadden			3	3	"	"	"
1552	56	5	28	Elizabeth Falconer					Alexander	Wardend Altyre	Half Davoch
1553	56	8	21	John Alex Calder					Alexander	Coulmony	
1554	56	8	21	Margaret McMillan Calder					"	"	
1555	56	8	21	Daisy Margach Stuart					William	Dounduff	None
1556	56	10	9	Heather Gammie					Mrs Gammie	Woodhead Logie	Half-Davoch
1557	56	10	31	William Scott					Robert	Blairs Farm Altyre	Rafford.
1558	56	11	26	Allistair Grant		45		1	Alex.	Mains of Sluie	Conicavel
1559	57	2	5	Shonagh Macaulay					c/o Macaulay, Forester	Cothall, Altyre.	West Africa
1560	57	4	23	Elizabeth Chalmers Ross					Alexander	Home Farm, Logie	None
1561	57	4	23	Alexandra E. Morrison		52			Alexander	Relugas Village	"
1562	57	4	23	Mary E. Geddie					Colin	Blairs Farm Altyre	"
1563	57	4	23	Jean A. MacLennan					Simon	" " "	"
1564	57	4	23	David M. Reid					William	Divie Lodge	"
1565	57	5	6	June Patricia Gammie					Mrs Gammie	Ardoch Cottage.	"
1566	57	8	20	Sheila Catherine Maclennan					Simon	Blairs Farm	"
1567	58	4	15	William Meldrum					William	Blairs Farm	"
1568	58	4	15	Catherine Mary Ross					Alexander	Home Farm, Logie	"
1569	58	4	15	Linda M. A. Grant			3	1	Donald	Relugas Village	"
1570	58	4	15	Robert John Geddie			3	27	Colin	Blairs Farm	"
1571	58	4	15	Hazel Agnes Noble					Donald	Cothall Cottage, Altyre	"
1572	58	4	15	Sheila Eliz. Taylor					Howie	Wardend Altyre	"
1573	58	4	15	Michael Alex Reid					William	Divie Lodge, Logie	"
1574	58	5	13	John Alex Calder					Alexander	Dounduff Cottages	Glenferness
1575	58	5	13	Margaret McMillan Calder					"	"	"
1576	58	6	16	Marjorie L. Raffle	1548				James	Logie P. O.	From Germany
1577	58	6	16	Maureen G. Robertson					James	The Offices, Altyre.	Braeside, Turriff
1578	58	6	16	Pearl Mary Robertson					"	"	"
1579	58	8	19	David Morrison					Alex.	Relugas	None.
1580	59	2	16	Heather Campbell					Mrs Campbell	Peatbillock	Inverness Central
1581	59	4	13	James Alex. Wilson					Edmond	The Offices, Altyre	Burgie.
1582	59	4	13	Dorothy C. Wilson					"	"	"
1583	59	4	13	John Ramach					John	Woodhead Logie	None.
1584	59	4	13	Ian Morris					Lawrence	Lower Cothall, Altyre	"
1585	59	4	13	Irene Geddie					Colin	Blairs "	"
1586	59	4	13	Christine M. McLennan					Simon	" "	"
1587	59	4	13	Caroline A. M. Scott					John	" "	"
1588	59	5	5	James Robertson					Innes	" "	Roseisle
1589	59	6	8	Georgina Helen Bowie					William	Cothall	Forres.
1590	59	6	8	Audrey Bowie					"	"	"
1591	59	8	25	Lorna Reid					William	Divie Lodge	None
1592	59	8	25	Donald Ross			31		William	Cothall, Altyre	None
1593	59	8	25	William Ross			12	31	"	"	Forres.
1594	59	8	25	Morris M. Grant			2	2	Charles	Coulmony	Cluny, Aberdeenshire
1595	59	9		Francis Michie	1535	41			Adam	Altyre	

Notes by Teacher and Signatures of School Managers with date of visit.

1590 Last entry by me as Headmaster James B. Pratt

1591 First entry by me on appointment as Headmaster. John C. Macisaac

WHETHER EXEMPTION FROM RELIGIOUS INSTRUCTION IS CLAIMED	The highest standard in which he was there presented, and the results of his last EXAMINATION				Class into which admitted	Showing the Successive Standards in which presented in this School, with date and result of examination.						Showing the Specific Subjects in which he was presented in his LAST and in THIS School.															EXACT DATE OF LEAVING			CAUSE OF LEAVING.
	St⁴	R	W	A		I	II	III.	IV.	V	VI	STANDARD V		STANDARD VII		STANDARD Ex.VI		STANDARD Ex.Ex.VI								Year	Month	Day	
																										57	8	20	Gone to Forres
																										56	4	24	GONE TO GERMANY
																										57	4	11	GONE TO KINLOCHLEVEN
																										57	4	11	"
																										57	4	11	"
																										57	8	20	Forres Academy.
																										56	10	1	Transferred to Glenferness
																										56	10	1	" " "
																										58	4	15	Gone to Forres
																										57	3	15	Returned to Africa.
																										64	7	1	Forres Academy
																										64	7	1	Forres Academy
																										"	"	"	"
																													To Keam.
																										64	7	1	Forres Academy
																										58	4	15	Gone to Forres
																													To Keam.
																										62	9	7	To Fife
																										65	7	1	Forres Academy.
																										65	7	1	" "
																										65	7	1	" "
																													Left District.
																										59	1	5	Gone to Forres
																										65	7	1	Forres Academy.
																										58	6	16	Gone to Dunphail
																													"
																										59	3	16	Gone to Aberdeenshire
																										59	3	16	"
																										65	7	1	Forres Academy.
																										59	3	26	Returned to Inverness
																										59	3	26	Returned to Inverness
																													Forres Academy
																										62	2	9	To Tomaveen, Aberdeenshire.
																										61	10	27	To Huntly
																										66	7	1	Forres Academy.
																													To Keam.
																													To Burgie.
																													Left District - Elgin.
																										67	7	1	Forres Academy.
																										6?			Forres Academy.
																										66	7	1	" "
																										62	1	12	Conicavel (Temp)
																										62	1	12	"
																										61	7	1	Nairn Academy
																										60	7	1	Forres Academy

SUCCESSIVE NUMBER (ON ADMISSION OR RE-ADMISSION)	DATE OF ADMISSION OR RE-ADMISSION			NAME IN FULL CHRISTIAN AND SURNAME.	IF RE-ADMITTED ORIGINAL ADMISSION NUMBER	EXACT DATE OF BIRTH			NAME AND ADDRESS OF PARENT OR GUARDIAN.		LAST SCHOOL ATTENDED BEFORE ENTERING THIS SCHOOL
	Year	Month	Day			Year	Month	Day			
1596	60	3	23	George A. King					Mrs Murdoch	Blairs Farm Cott, Altyre	Burghead.
1597	60	3	23	Thomas William King					" "	" " "	Roseisle.
1598	60	3	23	Norman King			3		" "	" " "	Roseisle.
1599	60	5	?	Pamela Graham				1?	George Graham	Coulmony Cottages	Culloden.
1600	60	8	23	William George Bowie			3		William Bowie	Cothall, Altyre	None
1601	60	8	23	James Mackenzie Falconer				7	James Falconer	Drumine	"
1602	60	8	23	Katrina Anne Macaulay			1	3	Grigor Macaulay	Cothall Hse, Altyre	"
1603	60	8	23	Rosemary Meldrum				8	William Meldrum	Blairs Farm, Altyre	"
1604	60	8	23	Diane May Murray					George Murray	Ardoch, Dunphail	"
1605	60	8	23	Alexander Charles Ross				13	Alexander Ross	Home Farm, Logie	"
1606	60	8	23	George Stuart				07	Mrs Stuart	Dounduff.	"
1607	60	8	23	Elizabeth McGillivray					William McGillivray	Craigroy, Dunphail	Half Davoch.
1608	60	8	23	Ena Dawson					Albert Dawson	Claschu, Dunphail	" "
1609	60	8	23	Linda Nicholson.					Donald Nicholson	Reypaul, Dunphail	" "
1610	60	8	23	Moray Ralph.			1	2	Ivor Ralph	Cowgreens, Dunphail	" "
1611	60	8	23	Graham McGillivray.					William McGillivray	Craigroy, Dunphail	" "
1612	60	8	23	Doreen Dawson.					Albert Dawson	Claschu Lodge, Dunphail	" "
1613	60	8	23	Alexander Moir.					William Moir	Tonnacroo, Dunphail	" "
1614	60	8	23	Gladys Elsie Dawson				8	Albert Dawson	Claschu Lodge, Dunphail	" "
1615	60	8	23	Ian William Grant					Edward Grant	Brachead, Logie	Dunphail.
1616	60	8	23	Margaret Wilson					Edmund Wilson	Blairs Farm Cott, Altyre	None
1617	60	10	18	Alexander Davidson					Alexander Davidson	Blain Farm Cotts, "	Huntly Gordon School
1618	60	11	14	Sheila Ritchie					Thomas Ritchie	Blairs Farm Cotts, "	Forres Primary
1619	60	11	28	Leonard Murray			11	13	Walter Murray	Greens Kennels, Dunphail	Cornhill, Banff
1620	61	2	27	Alistair Innes			1	1	Alexander Innes	Blairs Farm, Altyre	Inchmore, Inverness
1621	61	2	27	May Innes					" "	" " "	" "
1622	61	2	27	Ronald Innes.		54			" "	" " "	" "
1623	61	2	27	Marion Innes		5	14		" "	" " "	" "
1624	61	3	13	John Hutcheon		54	4	4	Harry Hutcheon	Easter Greens.	Glenogilvy Angus
1625	61	5	29	Douglas Milne.		52	12	12	Mrs Milne	Cothall, Altyre	Drummie Crieff
1626	61	5	29	Gordon Milne.					" "	" "	Gordon College
1627	61	8	31	Gordon Innes				7	Mrs Innes	Blain Cotts, Altyre	Rothiemay
1628	61	8	31	John Innes.					Mrs Innes	Blain Farm, Altyre	"
1629	61	8	31	James Andrews				2	William Andrews	Blain Farm Cott, Altyre	Alves
1630	61	8	31	Sheena Holland				3	Mrs Goodfellow	Relugas	Ballater
1631	61	8	31	Sheila Rutherford					Mrs Reid.	Divie Lodge, Logie	None
1632	61	8	31	Heather Fawson					David Fawson	West Lodge, Relugas	"
1633	61	8	31	Alison McGillivray					William McGillivray	Craigroy, Dunphail	"
1634	61	8	31	Evelyn Michie			5	4	Adam Michie	Blain Farm, Altyre	"
1635	61	8	31	Sheila Morris			6	1	Laurence Morris	Cothall, Altyre	"
1636	61	8	31	Elizabeth Wilson		5	12	1	John Wilson	Cothall, Altyre	"
1637	61	8	31	Norman Greig.		5			Alex. Greig.	Blain Farm, Altyre	"
1638	61	8	31	Alan Larnach		5			John Larnach	Woodhead, Logie	"
1639	61	8	31	Grant Nicholson			2	2	Donald Nicholson	Reypaul, Dunphail	"
1640	61	8	31	John Ross.			5	3	William Ross	Cothall, Altyre	"
1641	61	8	31	Graham Taylor		5			James Taylor	County Cotts, Logie	"
1642	62	1	3	James M. Falconer	1601	5		7	James Falconer	Drumine.	Fornighty
1643	62	2	12	John Ross.	1640	5	5		William Ross	Cothall, Altyre	Conicavel.
1644	62	2	12	Donald Ross.	1592	4	49	3	" "	" "	"
1645	62	2	12	William Ross.	1593	47	11	31	" "	" "	"

Notes by Teacher and Signatures of School Managers with date of visit.

WHETHER EXEMPTION FROM RELIGIOUS INSTRUCTION IS CLAIMED	The highest standard in which he was there presented, and the results of his last EXAMINATION			Class into which admitted	Showing the Successive Standards in which presented in this School, with date and result of examination						Showing the Specific Subjects in which he was presented in his LAST and in THIS School.													EXACT DATE OF LEAVING			CAUSE OF LEAVING.
	Std	R	W	A		I	II	III	IV	V	VI	STANDARD V	STANDARD VI	STANDARD Ex. VI	STANDARD Ex. Ex. VI								Year	Month	Day	
																							60	7	1	To Forres Academy
																							61	10	13	To Burghead.
																							61	10	13	"
																							63	3	29	To Inverness.
																										To Dunphail
																										To Fornighty
																							67	7	1	To Forres Academy.
																							62	9	7	To Fife.
																							67	7	1	To Forres Academy
																							"	"	"	" "
																							"	"	"	" "
																							"	"	"	" "
																							66	7	1	Forres Academy
																							66	7	1	" "
																										To Portsmouth.
																							65	7	1	Forres Academy.
																							62	7	12	Forres Academy.
																							61	7	1	" "
																							62	7	12	" "
																							66			Removed to Rothes
																							60	12	23	Parents left District
																							63	7	5	Forres Academy.
																							63	3	22	To Knockando
																							1	7	62	To Forres Academy.
																							63	3	29	To Findhorn.
																							63	3	29	" "
																							63	3	29	" "
																							62	7	12	Forres Academy
																										gone to Newhaystie
																							61	7	12	Gordon's College.
																							61	11	17	To Rothiemay.
																							61	11	17	" "
																							65	7	1	Forres Academy.
																							65	7	1	" "
																							62	11	17	To Banchory
																							63	3	22	To Nottingham, England
																							68	6	28	To Forres Academy.
																							"	"	"	To Forres Pr. (Special Class)
																							61	10	27	To Huntly
																							62	3	16	To Bungie
																										To Inverness-shire
																							62	2	9	To Tornaveen.
																							68	6	28	To Forres Academy
																										To Forres Primary School
																							68	6	28	To Forres Academy.
																							63	1	18	To Fornighty.
																										To Forres Primary School
																							66	7	1	Forres Academy
																							62	7	1	To Forres Academy.

Successive Number (on admission or re-admission)	Date of admission or re-admission Year	Month	Day	NAME IN FULL CHRISTIAN AND SURNAME	If re-admitted original admission number	Exact date of birth Year	Month	Day	NAME AND ADDRESS OF PARENT OR GUARDIAN		LAST SCHOOL ATTENDED BEFORE ENTERING THIS SCHOOL
1646	62	2	12	Douglas Milne	1625	15	12	12	Mrs Milne	Cothall, Altyre	Carnoustie
1647	62	4	16	Linda Mary Paton			12	4	George Paton	County Cotts, Logie	Rafford
1648	62	4	16	Brenda Jane Paton				3	"	"	"
1649	62	4	23	George Paton			1	1	"	"	"
1650	62	4	23	Penelope Riddoch			3	2	George Riddoch	Blairs Farm, Altyre	Alford, Aberdeen
1651	62	5	8	George Riddoch			3	1	"	"	"
1652	62	8	30	Hamish Philip Anderson			7		Alastair Anderson	Outlawell, Logie	None
1653	62	8	30	Fiona Shirah Grant			7	2	Alexander Grant	Servally Cott, Relugas	"
1654	62	8	30	George Grant			9	9	Edward Grant	Brachead, Logie	"
1655	62	8	30	Stephen Reid			6	10	William Reid	Divie Lodge	"
1656	62	8	30	John Roderick Ross			11	16	Alexander Ross	Home Farm, Logie	"
1657	62	10	22	Katharine Mary Packwood			5	11	Mrs Packwood	Presley Cott, Logie	Convent School, Nairn
1658	63	3	26	Pauline Turek			4	3	Paul Turek	Greens Kennels, Dunphail	Rafford
1659	63	3	26	Paul Turek	1625 1646		4	12	Paul Turek	Greens Kennels, Dunphail	"
1660	63	4	29	Douglas Milne			12	12	Mrs Milne	Cothall, Altyre	Malaya
1661	63	6	17	Neil Mutch			6	2	William Mutch	West Lodge, Relugas	Braeside, Auchnagatt
1662	63	8	27	Margaret Mary Burr			7	5	Andrew Burr	Daltullich Farm, Dunphail	"
1663	63	8	27	Sheila Evelyn Burr			12	3	"	"	"
1664	63	8	27	Alan Dawson			2		Mrs Dawson	Clashduhn, Dunphail	None
1665	63	8	27	Charles Ewan			55	6	Archibald Ewan	Blair Farm, Altyre	"
1666	63	8	27	Bruce McGillivray			8	31	William McGillivray	Craigroy, Dunphail	"
1667	63	8	27	Lesley J. Mutch			5	51	William Mutch	West Lodge, Relugas	"
1668	63	8	27	Marianne Nicolson			8	5	Donald Nicolson	Regaul, Dunphail	"
1669	63	8	27	Nancy Nicolson			5	2	Stewart Nicolson	Relugas Mains	"
1670	63	8	27	Alison Packwood			7	1	Edward Packwood	Presley Cott, Logie	"
1671	63	8	27	David J. Ross			16	12	Alex. Ross	Home Farm, Logie	"
1672	63	8	27	Patricia Stuart			1	1	Mrs Stuart	Dounduff	"
1673	63	8	27	Marilyn Thomson			6	9	William Thomson	Blairs Farm, Altyre	"
1674	64	8	25	John J. Bremner			12		John Bremner	Tornamoon	"
1675	64	8	25	Robert Yeats Gerrard			3	2	Mrs Gerrard	Blairs Farm, Altyre	"
1676	64	8	25	Brian Macleod			2	2	William Macleod	Peathillock, Logie	"
1677	64	8	25	Michael John Mitchell			8	6	Alan Mitchell	Cothall Cotts, Altyre	"
1678	64	8	25	John Nicolson			10	10	Stewart Nicolson	Relugas Mains	"
1679	64	8	25	Edward Paton			1	6	George Paton	County Houses, Logie	"
1680	64	8	25	Lorna Aline MacDonald			7	10	George MacDonald	Muir of Logie Cott	"
1681	64	8	25	Morag MacPherson			7	5	James MacPherson	West Lodge, Altyre	"
1682	64	8	25	Gail Nicolson			5	11	Carol Nicolson	Relugas Mains Cott	"
1683	64	9	22	Janet G. Duncan			2	11	Robert Duncan	Balinreach	Thornbryde
1684	64	9	22	Michael S. Duncan					" "	Balinreach	"
1685	64	10	20	Raymond Strachan			4	12	John Strachan	Cothall Cott	Fyvie
1686	64	11	30	Andrew Watt			4	11	Andrew Watt	The Gardens, Altyre	Forres Primary
1687	65	1	5	Graham Shanks			11	1	Peter Shanks	Wester Regaul	Dunphail
1688	65	1	5	Gordon Shanks			7	10	"	"	"
1689	65	8	24	Marshi Bremner				10	John Bremner	Tornamoon	None
1690	65	8	24	Lesley Ross				1	William Ross	Blairs Farm Cott	"
1691	65	8	24	Jamie Duncan			10		Robert Duncan	Balinreach	"
1692	65	8	24	Pam MacPherson			1	9	Mrs McPherson	West Lodge, Altyre	"
1693	65	8	24	Ronald Grant			10	9	Alex Grant	Relugas	Forres
1694	65	11	25	Evelyn Jane Duncan			5	52	Alex Duncan	Ardoch	Fornighty
1695	65	11	25	William George Duncan			3	11	" "	"	"

Notes by Teacher and
Signatures of School Managers
with date of visit.

WHETHER EXEMPTION FROM RELIGIOUS INSTRUCTION IS CLAIMED	The highest standard in which he was there presented and the results of his last EXAMINATION				Class into which admitted	Showing the Successive Standards in which presented in this School, with date and result of examination.						Showing the Specific Subjects in which he was presented in his LAST and in THIS School. STANDARD V			STANDARD VII			STANDARD Ex.VI			STANDARD Ex.Ex.VI			EXACT DATE OF LEAVING			CAUSE OF LEAVING.
	St.d	R.	W.	A.		I	II	III.	IV.	V	VI													Year	Month	Day	
																								63	7	5	To Gordon's College
																								64	7	1	Forres Academy.
																								65	7	1	„ „
																								65	12	3.	Kinloss.
																											Forres Academy.
																								68	6	28	Forres Academy.
																											To Glenferness.
																											To Forres Academy.
																											„ „
																											„ „
																											To Forres P. School
																								68	10	15	Binbrook C of E. Sch. Lincs.
																											To Perthshire.
																								63	7	5	To Gordon's College.
																								65	7	1	To Aberdeenshire
																											To Glenferness
																											„ „
																								70	7	1	To Forres Academy.
																								70	7	1	„ „ „
																								71	7	2	Forres Academy.
																								65	7	1	Turriff.
																								70	7	1	To Forres Academy.
																								70	7	1	To Forres Academy
																								68	10	15	Binbrook R.A.F. Lincs
																											To Forres P. School
																								71	7	2	Forres Academy
																								69	12	23	To Bishopmill P.S. Elgin.
																								71	7	2	To Forres Academy
																											To Inverness-shire.
																								71	7	2	To Forres Academy
																											To Edinburgh.
																								71	7	2	To Forres Academy
																								65	12	3.	Kinloss.
																								71	7	2	Forres Academy
																								71	7	2	„ „
																								71	7	2	„ „
																								65	7	1	Forres Academy.
																											To Bridge of Marnoch
																											To Forres Academy.
																								66	7	1	Forres Academy
																								66	7	1	„ „
																											Forres Academy.
																								71	6	8	Biggar, Lanarkshire
																								72	6	30	Forres Academy
																											To Bridge of Marnoch, Banffshire
																								72	6	30	To Forres Academy
																								72	6	30	To Forres Academy
																								67	7	1	To Forres Academy.
																											„ „

SUCCESSIVE NUMBER (ON ADMISSION OR RE-ADMISSION)	DATE OF ADMISSION OR RE-ADMISSION			NAME IN FULL CHRISTIAN AND SURNAME.	IF RE-ADMITTED ORIGINAL ADMISSION NUMBER	EXACT DATE OF BIRTH.			NAME AND ADDRESS OF PARENT OR GUARDIAN.		LAST SCHOOL ATTENDED BEFORE ENTERING THIS SCHOOL
	Year	Month	Day			Year	Month	Day			
1696	65	11	25	Gilbert James Duncan		56	11	17	Alex Duncan	Ardoch, Dunphail	Fornighty.
1697	66	5	16	Evelyn Ross		56	1	1	Mrs Ramage	Daltullich Farm	Avoch.
1698	66	5	16	Whilelmina Ross.		56	6	5	" "	" "	Avoch.
1699	66	8	23	Adaelinn Joan Bremner				53	Mrs Bremner	South Lodge, Dunphail	Auchinblae.
1700	66	8	23	Darra Campbell.				51	Alex Campbell.	Feakirk, Dunphail	Dunphail.
1701	66	8	23	Steven Charles Foss		5		11	Mrs Allan.	The Gardens, Dunphail	"
1702	66	8	23	Roderick J. Mackenzie		5			Robt Mackenzie	Balblair Cott, Dunphail	"
1703	66	8	23	Arthur Sorrie		54		6	Arthur Sorrie	Home Farm, Dunphail	"
1704	66	8	23	Brian Sorrie		56		11	" "	" "	"
1705	66	8	23	Donald Mackenzie.		50	10	10	Robt Mackenzie	Balblair Cott, Dunphail	"
1706	66	8	23	Colin Campbell.		57	13	13	Alex Campbell.	Feakirk, Dunphail	"
1707	66	8	23	Graham Calder		57			George Calder	Post Office, Dunphail	"
1708	66	8	23	Frank Pratt.		57	6	1	George Pratt.	The Garage, Dunphail	"
1709	66	8	23	Kenneth Sorrie.		58			Arthur Sorrie	Home Farm, Dunphail	"
1710	66	8	23	Stephen George Fraser		60			Ronald Fraser.	Glenernie Farm, Dunphail	"
1711	66	8	23	Joseph James Crilley		60	5	3	Joseph Crilley.	Gordhu Cott, Dunphail	"
1712	66	8	23	Spencer John Foss		60	11		Mrs Allan	The Gardens, Dunphail	"
1713	66	8	23	Haydn Melville Foss		61			" "	" "	"
1714	66	8	23	Helen Robertson.		61			Roy Robertson	The Gardens, Dunphail	"
1715	66	8	23	Donelle Clark		3	1	61	Duncan Clark	Council Houses, Dunphail	"
1716	66	8	23	Catriona MacDonald.		61	2		John MacDonald.	Beachans, Dunphail	"
1717	66	8	23	Linda Evelyn Sorrie		61	11		Arthur Sorrie	Home Farm, Dunphail	"
1718	66	8	23	Alaistair Mair		61			John Mair	Schoolhouse, Half Davoch	None
1719	66	8	23	William Thomas Pretswell		66		1	William Pretswell	Relugas Mill, Relugas	"
1720	66	8	23	Fiona Campbell		60	10	10	Margaret Campbell	North Lodge, Logie.	"
1721	66	8	23	Lorraine Cowan.		61			Alexander Cowan	Wester Tullyglens.	"
1722	66	8	23	Maureen MacGillivray		61		11	William MacGillivray	Craigroy, Dunphail	"
1723	66	8	23	Audrey Margt Anne Pratt		61			George Pratt	The Garage, Dunphail	"
1724	67	4	12	Elizabeth Hamilton Ross	R. R.	58	1	1	William Ross	Cothall.	"
1725	67	4	12	Allan Thomas Nicolson		61			Stuart Nicolson	Relugas Mains	"
1726	67	4	12	David John Nicolson		62	11		Donald Nicolson	Relugas.	"
1727	67	5	22	Lorna Jean Ross.		61		11	John Ross	Daltullich Farm	Petty.
1728	67	5	22	David Francis Ross.		60			" "	" "	"
1729	67	5	22	Ann Margaret Ross.		55	1	31	" "	" "	"
1730	67	5	22	Alex John Ross.		52	2	13	" "	" "	"
1731	67	8	22	Charles Cowan		62	12	26	Alexander Cowan	West Tullyglens	None.
1732	67	8	22	Owen Goodfellow		61		1	Lewis Goodfellow	Relugas Village	"
1733	67	8	22	Kirstin Campbell.		61	3		Rev. Keith Campbell	Edinkillie Manse	"
1734	67	8	22	Beverley Craig.		61			Robert Craig.	1 Office Cottages, Altyre	"
1735	67	8	23	Shona Macdonald		62	11	21	John Macdonald	Beachans Cott, Dunphail	"
1736	67	8	22	David Allan Ross		62	11	11	Allan Ross	Divie Brae, Dunphail	"
1737	67	12	11	John Taylor.		61	11	1	Charles Taylor	Logie Home Farm	Llanbryde
1738	67	12	11	Stuart Taylor		63	11	11	"	Logie Home Farm	"
1739	68	1	29	Allan Lorimer MacHattie		62	1	1	William MacHattie	Cothall Cott, Altyre	Elgin East End
1740	68	1	29	William Joseph MacHattie		63		3	"	" "	"
1741	68	4	29	Sheena McCallum		61			Gilbert McCallum	Gardener's Cott, Logie	Fife
1742	68	5	7	George Brands.		56	6	7	Jack Brands,	Beachans Cott, Dunphail	Trossker, Cornwall
1743	68	8	20	Gavin Smith		60	6	7	Alfred Smith.	The Kennels, Glenernie	Dochgarroy, Inverness
1744	68	8	20	James F. Smith		62	2	1	" "	"	" "
1745	68	8	20	Alfred Ewan Smith		64	12	12	" "	"	" "

Notes by Teacher and
Signatures of School Managers
with date of visit.

WHETHER EXEMPTION FROM RELIGIOUS INSTRUCTION IS CLAIMED	The highest standard in which he was there presented, and the results of his last EXAMINATION				Class into which admitted	Showing the Successive Standards in which presented in this School with date and result of examination.						Showing the Specific Subjects in which he was presented in his LAST and in THIS School.																					EXACT DATE OF LEAVING			CAUSE OF LEAVING.
	St⁴	R.	W.	A.		I	II	III	IV.	V	VI																					Year	Month	Day	
																																70	7	1	Forres Academy.
																																66	4	1	To Nairn Academy.
																																			To Milbank P. School, Nairn
																																68	6	28	To Forres Academy
																																"	"	"	
																																"	"	"	Wiltshire.
																																"	"	"	To Forres Academy.
																																"	"	"	
																																			To Insch, Aberdeenshire
																																			Forres Academy.
																																			"
																																			Forres Primary.
																																70	7	1	Forres Academy.
																																			Insch, Aberdeenshire
																																72	6	30	Forres Academy
																																67	7	1	To Dyke.
																																68	6	28	Moved to Wiltshire.
																																"	"	"	" " "
																																			Forres Academy.
																																70	7	1	Forres Academy.
																																71	7	2	Forres Academy
																																			Insch, Aberdeenshire
																																66			To Rafford.
																																70	4	7	Forres Pr. (Special Class)
																																73	6	29	Forres Academy.
																																			Moved to Fife.
																																73	6	29	Forres Academy
																																73	6	29	Forres Academy
																																			Forres Primary School.
																																74	6	28	Forres Academy
																																74	6	28	Forres Academy
																																68	6	28	To Conon.
																																"	"	"	"
																																"	"	"	"
																																"	"	"	"
																																			Moved to Fife
																																74	6	28	Forres Academy
																																68			To Broughty Ferry.
																																			Moved to Kent
																																72	2	18	To Forres
																																			To Forres P. School
																																			To Banffshire.
																																			"
																																			To Elgin East End.
																																69	12	23	" " "
																																			To Alves.
																																			To Forres Academy
																																			To Farland, Aberdeenshire
																																			" "

SUCCESSIVE NUMBER (ON ADMISSION OR RE-ADMISSION)	DATE OF ADMISSION OR RE-ADMISSION			NAME IN FULL CHRISTIAN AND SURNAME	IF RE-ADMITTED ORIGINAL ADMISSION NUMBER	EXACT DATE OF BIRTH.			NAME AND ADDRESS OF PARENT OR GUARDIAN.		LAST SCHOOL ATTENDED BEFORE ENTERING THIS SCHOOL.
	Year	Month	Day			Year	Month	Day			
1746	68	8	20	Colin Hugh Kidd		63		4	Hugh Kidd	Logie Home Farm	None
1747	68	8	20	David Sinclair Reid			11	11	Roy Reid	Wester Tullyglens	"
1748	68	8	20	Russell Reid				31	William Reid	Post Office, Logie	"
1749	68	8	20	Norman Taylor				24	Charles Taylor	Logie Home Farm	"
1750	68	8	20	Rozanne Adele Clark				3	Duncan Clark	County Houses Dunphail	"
1751	68	8	20	Yvonne Coutts				2	James Coutts	Beachans Cotts "	"
1752	68	8	20	Denise Duguid				8	John Duguid	Cothall Cotts, Altyre	"
1753	68	8	20	Suzanne M. Ewan			7	2	Archibald Ewan	Blairs Farm, Altyre	"
1754	68	8	20	Carol Ann Young		188	8	0	Alistair Young	Blackloch, Logie	"
1755	69	8	26	Robert John Boag		6		11	Colin Boag	Schoolhouse, Half Davoch	"
1756	69	8	26	Irene Brands		6		2	Jack Brands	Beachans Cott, Dunphail	"
1757	69	8	26	Alasdair Gordon Chalmers		6		11	Iain G. Chalmers	Relugas House, Relugas	"
1758	69	8	26	William Scott Ferguson		6		2	Ian Ferguson	Dunphail Mains	"
1759	69	8	26	Roy Douglas Fraser		6		K	Ronald Fraser	Glenernie Farm Dunphail	"
1760	69	8	26	Ian Gray		6		1	Hugh Gray	Home Farm, Logie	"
1761	69	8	26	Douglas W.S. Goss		6		2	David Goss	Auchnagairn, Relugas	"
1762	69	8	26	Michael Stewart Goss		10	10	0	"	" "	Jedburgh GS
1763	69	8	26	David Gillanders		10	2	14	Gordon Gillanders	Cothall Cotts Altyre	None
1764	69	8	26	Janice Kidd		6		5	Hugh Kidd	Home Farm Cotts Logie	"
1765	69	8	26	Allan James Michie		6		2	Adam Michie	Blairs Farm Cotts Altyre	"
1766	69	8	26	Neil McDonald		6		5	John McDonald	Moss-side, Logie	"
1767	69	8	26	Robert Grant Morrison		64		32	Alex Morrison	Relugas Village	"
1768	69	8	26	James Fraser Simpson		6		12	James Simpson	Tullyglens, Dunphail	"
1769	69	8	26	Wendy Strachan		62	12	12	John Strachan	Cothall Cott, Altyre	"
1770	69	8	26	Linda Mielewczyk		63	7	17	Wladislaw Mielewczyk	Home Farm, Logie	Dyke
1771	69	8	26	Michael Mielewczyk		62	6	2	"	" " "	"
1772	69	11	10	Doreen Duff		62		4	David Duff	Hom Farm, Dunphail	Maryhawk, Ross-shire
1773	69	12	15	Ian Michael Downie		60	9	9	Allen Downie	Outlawell, Logie	N. Weald
1774	69	12	15	Edwin Vay Houston		60	5	9	Stanley Houston	South Lodge, Dunphail	Forres P.
1775	69	12	15	Alistair Galt Houston		63	10	10	"	" "	"
1776	69	12	15	Kathleen Annabella Houston		6	1	7	"	" "	"
1777	70	1	5	Sandra Grant		66	5	5	Alex Grant	Blairs Farm, Altyre	Alves
1778	70	1	5	Shaun Read		66	10	11	"	" "	"
1779	70	1	5	Sharon Read		67	1		"	"	"
1780	70	8	25	John Fairlie Ferguson		6			John Ferguson	Dunphail Mains	None
1781	70	8	25	James Grant		6	2	2	Alex Grant	Altyre Gardens	None
1782	70	8	25	Philip Mielewczyk		67	1	9	Wladislaw Mielewczyk	Logie Farm	None
1783	70	8	25	Andrew Munro		6	1	30	David Munro Beachans	Beachan Farm Dunphail	None
1784	70	8	25	Gordon Nicolson		6		1	Charles Nicolson	Relugas Farm Cottages	None
1785	70	8	25	David Allan Wallace		6		2	James Wallace	Cothall Cottages, Altyre	None
1786	70	8	25	James Wallace		6		21	"	" "	Aboyne Academy
1787	70	8	25	Patricia Wallace		6		21	" "	" "	Aboyne Academy
1788	70	8	25	Michael Wallace		6			" "	" "	Aboyne Academy
1789	70	8	25	Keith Young		6		12	William Young	The Schoolhouse, Logie	Forres Primary
1790	70	8	25	Alistair Young		6		5	Alistair Young	Blackloch Logie	None
1791	70	8	25	Kevin Young		10	1			No. 1 Dorman Anyelew Relugas	None
1792	70	8	25	Lorraine Coutts		02	4	11	James Coutts	Beachans Cotts Dunphail	None
1793	70	8	25	Margaret McIntosh		6	2	12	William McIntosh	Sluie, Logie	None
1794	70	8	25	Heather Pretswell		6			William Pretswell	Relugas Mill	None
1795	70	8	25	Joan Isobel MacPherson		65	5	15	Mrs MacPherson	Altyre Lodge	None

Notes by Teacher and Signatures of School Managers with date of visit.

1779. Last entry made by me as Headmaster. John A. Maciver.
1780. First entry made by me as Headmaster. W.J. Young.

WHETHER EXEMPTION FROM RELIGIOUS INSTRUCTION IS CLAIMED	The highest standard in which he was there presented; and the results of his last EXAMINATION				Class into which admitted	Showing the Successive Standards in which presented in this School, with date and result of examination.						Showing the Specific Subjects in which he was presented in his LAST and in THIS School.																EXACT DATE OF LEAVING			CAUSE OF LEAVING.
	St⁴	R	W	A		I	II	III	IV	V	VI	STD V		STD VI		STD Ex VI		STD Ex Ex VI									Year	Month	Day	
																											73	6	29	To Life
																											75	7	4	To Forest Academy
																														To Banffshire
																											75	7	4	To Forest Academy
																											75	7	4	To Forest Academy
																											29	5	29	To Mosstowie
																											75	7	4	To Forest Academy
																											75	7	4	
																											76	7	1	To Forest Academy
																											76	7	1	Forest Academy
																											41	12	23	To Private School
																											72	6	30	To Applegrove
																											76	7	1	Forest Academy
																														Renfrewshire
																														Lhanbryde
																											42	11	3	To Glenferness
																											76	7	1	Forest Academy
																											72	2	7	To Forres
																											76	7	1	Forest Academy
																											77	7	1	Forest Academy
																											70	3	6	Renfrewshire
																											70	7	1	To Forest Academy
																											73	6	29	Forest Academy
																											75	7	4	" "
																											70	2	27	To Millbank Ps Nairn
																														To Banffshire
																											73	6	29	Forest Academy
																											73	6	29	Forest Academy
																											75	7	4	" "
																											72	6	30	To Applegrove
																											77	7	1	To Forest Academy
																											77	7	1	To Forest Academy
																											78	7	1	To Forest Academy
																											76	1	77	To Forest Applegrove
																											72	6	30	Forest Academy
																											73	6	29	Forest Academy
																											75	7	4	"
																											74	6	28	Forest Academy
																											77	7	1	Forest Academy
																											41	11	26	To Aberdeen
																											77	7	1	Forest Academy
																											72	12	29	Died 29 Dec
																											72	6	6	To Anderson's Forres
																											77	7	1	Forest Academy

Successive Number	Date of Admission or Re-admission Year	Month	Day	Name in Full Christian and Surname	If Re-admitted Original Admission Number	Exact Date of Birth Year	Month	Day	Name and Address of Parent or Guardian		Last School Attended Before Entering This School
1496	70	8	25	Morag Reid		6		2	Roy Reid	West Tillyglens	None
1497	70	9	14	Ian Elmslie					Sandra Hosie	West Tillyglens	Gorse O'Neill
1498	70	10	21	Robert Bremner		62			Wm Bremner	Logie Home Farm	Meek
1799	70	10	21	Sheila Bremner		12		2	Wm Bremner	Logie Home Farm	Meek
1800	71	6	8	Aileen Clarke				10	Mrs Clarke	St Blairs Farm	Forres Primary
1801	71	6	14	Diane Glass		14	12	42		Cothall Cottage	Aviemore
1802	71	6	14	Gary Glass						Cothall Cottage	Aviemore
1803	71	8	23	Kenneth Boag				23	Colin Boag	Half-Davoch Schoolhouse	None
1804	71	8	23	Patrick Chalmers		15		55	Iain Chalmers	Relugas House	None
1805	71	8	23	David Kidd		5	8	2	Hugh Kidd	Logie Home Farm	None
1806	71	8	23	Ian Reid				12	Roy Reid	Dorran House, Dunphail	None
1807	71	8	23	Susan Duff					David Duff	Home Farm, Dunphail	None
1808	71	8	23	Marie Enslie		4			Sandra Hosie	Wester Tillyglens	None
1809	71	8	23	Jane Ferguson		2	4		John Ferguson	Dunphail Mains	None
1810	71	8	23	Catriona Chalmers		10			Iain Chalmers	Relugas House	Private School, Altyre
1811	71	8	23	Emma Chalmers		12		9	Iain Chalmers	Relugas House	Private School, Altyre
1812	71	12	6	Sylvia Robertson					Alan Robertson	Avriel Cottage, Dunphail	Culcairn School, Udny
1813	71	12	6	Alan Robertson					"	Avriel Cottage, Dunphail	Culcairn School, Udny
1814	72	1	24	Christine Copland					Mrs Copland	Culfearn	Nairn High School
1815	72	1	24	Sharon Copland					"	Culfearn	Nairn High School
1816	72	2	8	Teresa Abbott		4		1	Mrs Abbott	Inver of Logie	
1817	72	2	8	Julie Abbott					"	"	
1818	72	5	15	Michael Horn		11	1	1	Mr Horn	4 County Houses	Applegrove
1819	72	9	1	Audrey Macdonald					Neil Macdonald	Gardeners House, Logie	
1820	72	9	1	Suzanne Gillanders		7			Gordon Gillanders	Cothall Cottage, Altyre	
1821	72	9	1	Brian Wallace					James Wallace	Cothall Cottages, Altyre	
1822	72	9	1	Russell Lelof						Cothall Cottage, Altyre	
1823	72	9	1	Stuart Enslie					Mrs Hosie	Wester Tillyglens	
1824	72	9	1	Wilma Mackintosh					Wm Mackintosh	Outlawwell Farm	
1825	72	9	5	Donald Ferguson				11	Donald Ferguson	Culnamy Mains	
1826	72	10	17	Colin Nicolson		63		3	Alex Nicolson	Glenferness Mains	Glenferness
1827	72	10	17	Heather Wilson		13		3	Hugh Wilson	The Kennels, Glenferness	Ferness
1828	72	10	17	Fiona Matheson		62			Ian Matheson	Achnahechan, Glenferness	Ferness
1829	72	10	17	Karl Taylor		34				Cothall Cottage	Liverpool
1830	73	4	3	Philip McDonald		15	15	40		The Stables, Dunphail	Lybster
1831	73	5	1	Amber Bineham		16			Mrs Bineham	4 Forestry Cottages, Ferness	Tonbridge, Kent
1832	73	5	1	Abigail Bineham		16			Mrs Bineham	"	Tonbridge, Kent
1833	73	5	14	Andrew James		11				Moss-side, Logie	Applegrove
1834	73	8	21	Gordon Wilson		14			Walter Wilson	Keeper's Cottage, Glenferness	Ferness
1835	73	8	21	Catriona Matheson		6	12	2	James Matheson	Achnahechan, Ferness	Ferness
1836	73	8	21	Catriona Macleod		11		10	William Macleod	Ferness Post Office	Ferness
1837	73	8	21	David Gillanders	1763	4		2	Gordon Gillanders		Ferness
1838	73	8	21	Andrew Watt		33			Mrs Watt	Wester Tillyglens	Portsoy
1839	73	8	21	Lorraine Watt		26			Mrs Watt	Wester Tillyglens	Portsoy
1840	73	8	21	Gary Hanton		19		3	John Hanton	Office Cottages, Altyre	
1841	73	8	21	Shirley Maclean				5		County Houses, Half Davoch	
1842	73	8	21	Jessie Nicolson					Stuart Nicolson	Relugas Mains	
1843	73	8	21	Audrey Geddie					Colin Geddie	Blairs Farm, Altyre	
1844	73	8	21	Patricia Geddie		16	6	16	Colin Geddie	Blairs Farm, Altyre	
1845	73	8	21	Roy Kidd		6	6	6	Hugh Kidd	Logie Home Farm	

Notes by Teacher and Signatures of School Managers with date of visit.

WHETHER EXEMPTION FROM RELIGIOUS INSTRUCTION IS CLAIMED	The highest standard in which he was there presented, and the results of his last EXAMINATION				Class into which admitted	Showing the Successive Standards in which presented in this School, with date and result of examination						Showing the Specific Subjects in which he was presented in his LAST and in THIS School.																EXACT DATE OF LEAVING			CAUSE OF LEAVING.
	Std	R	W	A		I	II	III	IV	V	VI															Year	Month	Day	
																										73	6	29	To Fife
																										71	4	2	Gone to Aberdeen (?)
																										70	12	23	Returned to Wick.
																										70	12	23	Returned to Wick.
																										71	4	2	Returned to Forres.
																										77	7	1	Forres Academy
																										78	7	1	Forres Academy
																										78	7	1	Forres Academy.
																										74	6	28	To Aberdeen Infirmary
																										78	7	1	Forres Academy
																										73	6	29	To Fife
																													Andersons Special School
																										73	1	29	To O'Neill Corse.
																										72	6	30	To Applegrove
																										72	6	30	To Forres Academy
																										74	6	28	Forres Academy.
																													To Malta
																													To Malta.
																										73	5	4	To Alness
																										73	5	4	To Alness.
																										73	2	28	To Seafield
																										73	2	28	To Seafield.
																										73	2	1	To Applegrove.
																										72	11	3	To Forness
																										74	1	77	To Forres & Applegrove.
																										73	1	29	To O'Neill Corse.
																										77	11	4	To Dyke
																										73	11	16	To Barthol Chapel, Aberdeen
																										75	7	4	Nairn Academy
																										75	7	4	Nairn Academy
																										75	7	4	To Nairn Academy
																										73	6	29	To Kinloss
																										73	6	1	To Crearlanish
																										73	6	29	To Nairn Academy
																										74	8	20	To London?
																										76	7	1	To Forres Academy
																										74	2	10	To Andersons Forres
																										75	10	17	To Auldearn
																										76	7	1	To Nairn Academy.
																										73	9	14	To Alves
																										73	9	14	To Alves.

57

Successive Number	Date of Admission			Name in Full (Christian and Surname)	If Re-admitted Original Admission Number	Exact Date of Birth			Name and Address of Parent or Guardian		Last School Attended before entering this school
	Year	Month	Day			Year	Month	Day			
1846	73	8	21	Paul Coutts		10			James Coutts	Knockfyffin, Dunphail	
1847	73	8	21	John White		6					Grangemouth
1848	73	9	24	Yvonne Hollywood		6			James Hollywood	The Stables, Dunphail	Hopeman
1849	73	10	16	Amanda Keil		7				West Tillyglens	Gollanfield
1850	73	10	16	Derek Keil		6				West Tillyglens	Gollanfield
1851	73	10	29	Ewan Hunter		4	14	19	James Hunter	Cornoch, Dunphail	Durham
1852	73	10	29	Andrew Hunter		6	4	2	" "	Cornoch, Dunphail	Durham
1853	73	12	3	Kevin Barry Gallaher		6		4	Tony Gallaher	Wordend, Altyre	Kiltarlity
1854	73	12	3	Paul John Gallaher		6			"	"	Kiltarlity
1855	73	12	3	Thomas Antony Gallaher		6			"	"	Kiltarlity
1856	73	12	3	Tracy Gallaher		4	4		"	"	Kiltarlity
1857	73	12	3	Catriona McLeod		60		22	Angus McLeod	2 Cottall Cottage, Altyre	Ballater
1858	73	12	3	George McLeod		60			"	"	"
1859	73	12	3	Norman McLeod		60	02		"	"	"
1860	74	1	7	Deborah Joan Pounder		6			Brian Pounder	Cothall Cottage, Altyre	Invernessshire
1861	74	1	7	James Murdo Pounder		6	4		"	"	
1862	74	2	18	Graham Allardes		6			Joe Allardes	Craigroy Cottage	Knockando
1863	74	2	18	Roger Allardes		6				Craigroy Cottage	Knockando
1864	74	8	20	Fiona Taylor					Ernest & Max		
1865	74	8	20	Alistair Nicolson					Alex Nicolson	Glenfenness mews	Glenfeness
1866	74	8	20	Rozanne Emilie Hosie		6S		2	Donald Hosie		
1867	74	8	20	Morag Robertson		5			Tom Robertson	The Kennels, Altyre	
1868	74	8	20	David Taylor					David Taylor	South Lodge, Logie	
1869	74	8	20	Scott Gordon		0			James Gordon	Greens Kennels, Dunphail	
1870	74	8	20	Graham Duff		6			David Duff	Dunphail mews	
1871	74	8	20	Carole Santer					Wm Santer	Blairs Farm	
1872	74	8	20	Michael Michie		6			Isobel Michie	5 Blairs Cottages, Altyre	
1873	74	8	20	Kevin Wallace		6	5		James Wallace	Cothall, Altyre	
1874	74	8	20	Michael Glass					Anne Glass	Bochan	
1875	74	10	22	Ewan Hunter		6			James Hunter	Bochan, Dunphail	Fort William
1876	74	10	22	Andrew Hunter		12	2		"	"	
1877	75	1	13	Iain Houseman		6			Marjorie Houseman	Dounduff Lodge	Malta
1878	75	1	13	Nicholas Houseman		6			Marjorie Houseman	Dounduff Lodge	Malta
1879	75	4	21	Bjørg Næssan		6		2	Mrs. Næssan	Muckle Lyne, Fness	Norway
1880	75	4	21	Mari Næssan		6			"	"	
1881	75	4	21	David O'Connor		15			Wm O'Connor	Culfearn, Dunphail	Alves P. School
1882	75	4	21	Maria O'Connor		6			"	"	
1883	75	8	19	Fresa Mackintosh					Wm	Outlawell	
1884	75	8	19	Roderick Wallace					James	Cothall, Altyre	
1885	75	8	19	Marilyn Simpson		10	10		James	Tillyglens, Dunphail	
1886	75	8	19	John Grant		0				Gardeners Cot., Altyre	
1887	75	8	19	Jacqueline Houseman			16	16	Margory	Dounduff Lodge	
1888	75	8	19	Caroline Thain		6				West Greens	
1889	75	8	19	Catherine Thain						West Greens	
1890	75	9	15	Karen Hardie		7	7	12	Robert	Gardener's Cottage, Relugas	St. Boswells
1891	75	9	15	Susan Hardie		13		13	Robert	Gardener's Cottage, Relugas	St. Boswells
1892	75	11	24	IAN GEORGE BLACK		18	1	22	IAN BLACK	SCHOOL HOUSE LOGIE	TIPPERTY NR. ELLON
1893	76	4	19	FIONA C. M. SWANSON		7			WILLIAM SWANSON	OLD STATION HOUSE DUNAGHIL	BLACKPOOL P. SCH. NEWTON ABBOTT
1894	76	8	18	JAMIE R. L. SWANSON		1	1	7	"	"	

Notes by Teacher and Signatures of School Managers with date of visit.

1891 Last entry by Headmaster W. J. Young
1892 First entry by Headmaster

	The highest standard in which he was there presented, and the results of his last EXAMINATION				Class into which admitted	Showing the Successive Standards in which presented in this School, with date and result of examination.						Showing the Specific Subjects in which he was presented in his LAST and in THIS School																	Exact Date of Leaving			Cause of Leaving
Whether exemption from religious instruction claimed	Std	R	W	A		I	II	III	IV	V	VI	STANDARD V		STANDARD VI		STANDARD Ex VI		STANDARD Ex Ex VI									Year	Month	Day	
																											73	8	31	
																											73	8	31	To Grangemouth
																											73	1	11	To Fife
																														To Fort William (Temporary)
																														To Fort William (")
																											74	6	28	Forres Academy
																											74	12	20	To Lossiemouth
																											74	12	20	
																											74	12	20	
																											73	6	14	To Dornoch
																											73	6	14	
																											74	1	6	To Andersons Special Class
																											74	12	6	To Hopeman
																											74	12	6	
																											78	7	1	Forres Academy
																											74	11	24	To
																											77	7	1	To Nairn Academy
																											75	4	14	To O'Neil Corse
																											75	2	21	To Nethybridge
																											24	1	77	To Forres Applegrove
																											77	7	1	Forres Academy
																											78	7	1	Forres Academy
																											75	8	29	To Campbeltown
																											75	8	29	To Campbeltown
																											3	7	75	To Nursery
																											3	7	75	
																											75	4	28	To Lossie
																											77	11	4	To Dyke
																											24	1	77	To Applegrove Forres
																											75	8	29	To Campbeltown
																											77	8	22	To Braemar
																											77	8	22	To Braemar
																											78	1	4	To Applegrove
																											5	1	77	To Saudi Arabia
																											5	1	77	To Saudi Arabia

SUCCESSIVE NUMBER (on admission or re-admission)	DATE OF ADMISSION OR RE-ADMISSION			NAME IN FULL CHRISTIAN AND SURNAME.	IF RE-ADMITTED ORIGINAL ADMISSION NUMBER	EXACT DATE OF BIRTH			NAME AND ADDRESS OF PARENT OR GUARDIAN.	LAST SCHOOL ATTENDED BEFORE ENTERING THIS SCHOOL
	Year	Month	Day			Year	Month	Day		
1895	76	8	18	NICOLA MACDONALD					NEIL MACDONALD	GARDENERS HSE LOGIE
1896	76	8	18	JULIE MUNRO			7	5	DAVID MUNRO	BEACHANS DUNPHAIL
1897	76	8	18	SARAH GRANT		5	7	7	ALEXANDER GRANT	TOWER COTTAGE ALTYRE
1898	76	8	18	DOUGLAS HOSIE		5	5		DONALD HOSIE	TOMBAIN DUNPHAIL
1899	76	8	18	ELIZABETH A. BLACK		71	1	7	IAN BLACK	SCHOOLHOUSE LOGIE
1900	77	3	7	LOUISE ANNE MORRIS		8			BARRY MORRIS	Upper Carnoch Cottage Dunphail	Applegrove, Forres
1901	77	3	7	CLAIRE ELAINE MORRIS		10	8	8	" "	"	"
1902	77	3	7	RICHARD JAMES MORRIS		4			" "	"	"
1903	77	8	24	MARCUS OLIVER WINDER		16			RON PARKER	THE DORRAN DUNPHAIL	BURLEY-IN-WHARFEDALE
1904	77	8	20	HAZEL-JANE WINDER				4	" "	" "	" "
1905	77	8	24	AVRIL MARGARET SOUTER			2	1	WILLIAM SOUTER	BLAIRS HOME FARM
1906	77	8	24	MAIRI DAWN MACLEAN		7	1	1	JAMES MACLEAN	TOMDHU DUNPHAIL
1907	77	8	24	SANDRA GLASS			7		MAGNUS GLASS	COTHALL COTTAGE ALTYRE
1908	77	8	24	CLAIRE ANNE GRANT				6	ALEXANDER GRANT	STABLES COTTAGE ALTYRE
1909	77	8	24	MALCOLM JAMES RENNIE				3	MRS. LESLEY RENNIE	POND COTTAGE ALTYRE
1910	77	8	20	SCOTT TAYLOR				3	DAVID TAYLOR	SOUTH LODGE LOGIE
1911	77	8	20	STEVEN JOHN YOUNG		7			ALISTAIR YOUNG	BLACKLOCH LOGIE
1912	77	8	24	NEIL WALKER MILLER		1		2	KATHLEEN	ARDOCH DUNPHAIL
1913	77	8	20	ROBERT ALEX. FARQUHAR		1	6	25	ROBERT FARQUHAR	BLAIRS ALTYRE
1914	77	8	24	JOSEPH ROBERT ALLARDES			15	25	GRAF JOSEPH ALLARDES	CRAIGROY DUNPHAIL
1915	77	8	24	NICOLA POWELL		6		11	DAVID POWELL	PRESLEY COTTAGE LOGIE
1916	77	9	9	SCOTT DOUGLAS		6		7	JAMES DOUGLAS	REUGAS GARDENS COTTAGE	WALLYFORD PRIMARY EAST LOTHIAN
1917	77	9	22	IAN HUXLEY		8			HARRY GORDON HUXLEY	TOMDHU DUNPHAIL	DALHOUSIE FORT RICHARDSON U.S.
1918	78	6	12	MICHAEL PERKINS		60	10		ELAINE PERKINS	NO. 4 STATION COTTAGES DUNPHAIL	- BORNEO
1919	78	8	22	JOHN ROBERTSON		65			THOMAS ROBERTSON	TOMBAIN DUNPHAIL	NEW PITSLIGO
1920	78	8	22	TOMMY ROBERTSON		7			THOMAS ROBERTSON	TOMBAIN DUNPHAIL	NEW PITSLIGO
1921	78	8	22	COLIN BURNS		7			MATTHEW BURNS	3 COTHALL COTTAGES
1922	78	8	22	JAMIE WHITTLE		2	2	2	COLIN WHITTLE	COTHALL ALTYRE
1923	78	8	22	MYLES HUNTER		37	3	7	JAMES HUNTER	BEACHANS COTTAGE DUNPHAIL
1924	78	5	15	IAN MACGREGOR		6			JOHN MACGREGOR	LOGIE HOME FARM	DYKEHEAD PENTSEY
1925	78	11	13	STEPHEN YOUNG		1	1		DAVID YOUNG	1 COTHALL COTTAGES	AVIEMORE PRIMARY
1926	78	11	13	DOUGLAS GRANT		6			IAIN GRANT	1 COTHALL COTTAGES	AVIEMORE
1927	78	11	24	THOMAS MCKENDRICK					THOMAS MCKENDRICK	LOGIE SCHOOLHOUSE	EDINBARNET SCHOOL CLYDEBANK
1928	79	4	23	Keith Robert Howard		2	0	10	CATHERINE HOWARD	BLAIRS FARM ALTYRE	SHEFFIELD
1929	21	8	79	PAUL DAVID MOFFIT			12	10	JOHN WIDDOWSON	5 COTHALL COTTAGES	DYKE
1930	21	8	79	CAINE LEE MOFFIT		76			JOHN WIDDOWSON	5 COTHALL COTTAGES
1931	21	8	79	MICHAEL RICHARD DUFF					BRIAN RICHARD DUFF	4 COUNTY COTTAGES
1932	21	8	79	ROBERT JOHN FRAZER		5	5	1	ROBERT FRAZER	WHITE HOUSE DUNPHAIL
1933	21	8	79	GORDON PHILIP GRANT				2	ALEXANDER GRANT	THE STABLES ALTYRE
1934	21	8	79	CHRISTOPHER JAMES MCKENDRICK					SCHOOL HOUSE LOGIE	SCHOOL HOUSE LOGIE
1935	21	8	79	JOHN MILLER			74		ARDOCH DUNPHAIL	KATHLEEN DUNCAN
1936	9	8	79	STEVEN THAIN					WESTERGREENS
1937	9	8	79	ZINNIA JANE WATT		14	7	1	THE GARDENS, ALTYRE	HEATHER DOREEN WATT

WHETHER EXEMPTION FROM RELIGIOUS INSTRUCTION CLAIMED	The highest standard in which he was there presented, and the results of his last EXAMINATION			Class into which admitted	Showing the Successive Standards in which presented in this School, with date and result of examination.						Showing the Specific Subjects in which he was presented in his LAST and in THIS School.																		EXACT DATE OF LEAVING			CAUSE OF LEAVING.
	Std	R.	W.	A.		I	II	III	IV	V	VI	STANDARD V		STANDARD VI		STANDARD Ex. VI		STANDARD Ex. Ex. VI										Year	Month	Day	
																												78	1	4	to Applegrove
																												78	10	3	To Cockermouth.
																												78	4	10	TO ARDGAY, SUTHERLAND
																												78	8	22	TO FORRES (Applegrove).
																												6.	4.	79	TO FORRES.

No: 1562, Mary Geddie, Altyre.

'We were loved and had plenty to eat..'

Blairs Home Farm • Mary E. Geddie

'Not the bus one again!' her daughter would laugh whenever she told it, but we all have our best stories and Mary's is a great one. In our minds we are both in the playground at Logie School and she's just been knocked over, but the main thing she can think about is her surprise that the headmaster is there in his slippers. From where she is lying with blood on her face, she can see the soap dripping off his. Mr Maciver had been shaving and dashed from his bathroom in the schoolhouse when he heard her sister Gwendoline shout for help.

She feels chilly on such a wet and windy day, there on the ground, but then if the weather had been better, she wouldn't have been hit at all. Geordie Calder always dropped the children at the bus shelter outside, but he'd felt sorry for them that day and driven right up to the school. He could turn at the top, he said.

Getting off the bus, Mary reckoned that she just had time before class to rush back to old Miss Robertson in the shop by the gate (or was she Mrs Robertson? She could somehow never picture a Mr). She was desperate to buy a little square pack of chewing gum, just for the card which came with it. And then maybe it was the wind or maybe she was just so excited, but she never heard the bus as it came back towards the road and now here she is, looking at the bumper from below, and she knows it was all her own fault. It was lucky, someone was saying, that Geordie was a good driver, or she'd have been under the wheel. He'd never bring the bus up to school again, he said, and he didn't.

Between them, Miss Robertson and Mr Maciver take her to the shop, placing her carefully on an old-fashioned sofa that she thinks they call a shades long. Dr Adam comes up from Forres, checks the cut on her temple and drives her home, and of course her parents are very sympathetic and say all the right things, and Geordie Calder comes by to check that she is fine. And then, when they have all gone, she gets a proper thrashing. That was just the way it was. They were right, she should have known better.

•

Mary's sense of responsibility did not stop there. She knew she should help out at home, with not much money to go round and (so far) three sisters and a brother: Gwendoline, Valerie, Robert and Irene, all to take their places in the register in turn. At twelve, determined not to wear a hand-me-down uniform to Forres Academy but to buy herself a brand-new one, Mary got a backbreaking job in the Altyre nursery, tweaking out the weeds. Mary and Valerie took charge of the family's tea too, setting the table, cooking the tatties, staving off hunger with sugar sprinkled on buttered bread and shaken off again.

She worked for a while at the Carlton and then left home at fifteen, going with her friend Irene Petrie to live and work at the Loirston Hotel in Ballater. It was there that she got a letter from her mother: she thought she was going through the change, she said, she was only 38 but she wasn't feeling so well. The next Mary heard, her mother – and she remembers the shock – was pregnant. Not as great a shock, I imagine, as the one her mother got a few months later in the labour ward in Inverness. The baby was born – a girl, premature but fine – but what was that the midwife was saying? 'Oh, Sheila, there's another one!' The Geddie twins had arrived.

Audrey and Patricia were six months old before Mary got to see them, with the hotel being so busy, but at least she had a boyfriend with a car who could come and fetch her and save her changing buses in Aberdeen and Elgin. Her father Colin, known as Ged, had worked his way up and kept pace with his growing family: starting as a plain farm worker, Mary tells me, he had moved to foreman and then to be grieve, before replacing Mr Souter as farm manager and becoming a good friend of Sir William Gordon Cumming, the men liking to walk the dogs round the loch together and catch up. The family's lives were entwined with the estate: Mary married (the boyfriend with the car) in the Scandinavian church and, in the end, when Ged died, Sir William asked her mother if she'd like him buried in the old Altyre cemetery. 'Thank you very much, but no,' she'd said. That place was too dark and eerie.

Her mother had a hard life – a phrase I hear often – working at the tatties, at the beating, in the Altyre nursery, at everything she could. Wages were not high but tatties were free and so was milk from the Altyre dairy, left in each worker's pail at the end of the day. And everyone, after all, was the same. The lunch at school was always two courses, so it didn't matter too much if tea at home was a stew with more vegetables than meat. The school lunch – meals like tattie jane, a dish of bacon, onion, veg and gravy, followed by 'fancy puddings' – was cooked by Mrs Mackenzie who lived in North Road and it was free for the poorer children. It's interesting that Mary can't remember, or never knew, if she was one of them.

Of course, they weren't the only big family on Altyre to go to Logie School: the Michies had five and so did the MacLennans. There were the Rosses and the Frasers and the Macphersons, the Meldrums and the Toughs, the Bowies, the Macaulays and other children at Cothall, too. 'Not many would say that they didn't have a happy childhood at Altyre,' says Mary. Everyone knew everything about each other there, she says, and I wonder for a moment which story she's thinking of. For a child, it was the get-togethers which stood out: guising round the houses at Halloween and a party at Christmas in the hall with presents for every family, and the New Year breakfasts when everyone landed at the Geddies.

I imagine that sense of community travelled with the children up to Logie School on the bus that went round the Half Davoch road, collecting the Patons and the Dawsons, the Macgillivrays and the Urquharts, the Nicolsons and Shanks and Grants. Mary lists the names as if counting heads on a day out. By this era, a dentist would bring his caravan to school, sending a letter home if you needed a tooth pulled, and a nurse would call with cod liver oil and to check for nits. In the classroom – today's school hall – the old fireplace and stove were there but had fallen out of use, but punishment most certainly hadn't. 'Mr Maciver thought I wasn't very bright,' says Mary. She was given the strap by him one day for cheating and copying Betty Ross (who was good at everything) when in fact she'd just been trying harder than usual. Her mother went up to school to complain and she never got picked on again.

But Mr and Mrs Maciver were lovely people, Mary says, and the measure of that was memory. When Mary worked at Brodie Countryfare, much later, after John and his wife had retired along the coast to Hopeman, Jean would always come over to where she was working in the shop and say hello: 'I remember you, Mary!' she'd say. Which maybe is what we all want, in the end, and explains why two sisters could have been seen crying one day in a newly converted building on Altyre. They had lived there once, but Mary and Tricia (half of the twin surprise) were hunting for some trace that they ever had. The kitchen, their granny's bedroom, the grain dryer, the byre, the dairy, the hay loft where they'd leapt from bales and swung from rafters, the red tiles polished with Cardinal by their mother – who, in the life that we know was hard, found time for that as well – and the little room kept for Mrs Wiseman, the milk recorder? 'There was nothing. We thought there would have been something but there was nothing up to tell you what it was like, what the people were like.' For a moment, though, I don't get what Mary means. I feel I know exactly who was there, what their lives had been like, and all because of the stories she's just been telling me.

No: 1652, Hamish Anderson, Outlawell.

'He'll not set the world on fire but you
won't get a more honest person..'

Outlawell • Hamish Philip Anderson

The story Hamish Anderson tells me is this. One morning, at some point in the 1980s, a man is shaving in the bathroom at Outlawell. Suddenly, in the mirror, he sees behind him a ghost with a disfigured face and ginger hair. The presence in the house is so terrible that they say the man's wife had a mental breakdown and word gets round that Outlawell is haunted. I later hear from others that people would cross themselves as they passed the farm and be fearful of venturing in alone.

To anyone who knew the Anderson family, who had lived in Outlawell for generations until the 1960s, there was an immediate and obvious answer. The ghost was a blend of two brothers, both in the Logie register: James Anderson, who was shot in the face in World War One, surviving but coming home seriously damaged, and red-haired Sandy, who suffered shell shock and later shot himself in the chest under the bridge at Mannachie.

Hamish Anderson is James' grandson and rang his Auntie Mary in Canada to discuss the ghost. Her response was practical, questioning not the existence of a ghost but rather who it might have been. 'It wouldn't be my father. He was a nice person. He wouldn't want to scare anybody.'

Hamish himself never knew his grandfather, who had died before he was born, and neither did he ever see a ghost at the house where he spent the first nine years of his life. His father Alastair had dreamt of joining the RAF but had been obliged to take on the farm, but his mother Margaret Philip came from farming stock at Alves and knew what she was taking on. They struggled to have children and suffered six miscarriages before Hamish was born. He was brought home to Outlawell only because his mother had spent six months in bed at Leanchoil.

The farm name, Hamish says, means 'well on the hill'. Others say that Outlawell was the limit of jurisdiction, the point at which lawbreakers were in the clear if heading south from Forres, but Hamish prefers his version. He remembers cranking the water up in pails before the days of the electric pump, being happy making butter and cheese with his mother, driving tractors before his legs were long enough to reach the pedals, his father a hair-raising risk-taker behind the wheel. Hamish loved it all.

And then his parents separated, Alastair leaving for Australia, his mother and her two boys leaving the farm and Hamish leaving Logie School.

•

Hamish has invited me to the house he lives in now, number 3, he's told me, and it's a surprise to find that he's called it Outlawell, after the farm. 'That's where the Andersons came from. It annoys me that it stopped in 1967 and I wish it had continued.' I notice that word 'annoys' and wonder if it's really enough. There was even a time when Hamish thought of moving back. 'Sometimes you have a wee dream. I thought it would be great to be there, but now I think what a stupid idea that was. You have to separate reality from fantasy.'

I've been spending some time trying to do that myself. It's impossible to imagine what people might have felt in unimaginable circumstances. When James had gone to the war, he'd left behind his 14-year-old sweetheart from the farm next door, Drumine. Jean Falconer was twelve years younger than the man she would go on to marry on his return, by then badly disfigured and for ever afterward turning his face from a camera.

'She doted on him,' says Hamish, and he says it was a happy marriage, the start of a trend among Anderson girls for choosing older men. It was Jean who was at the heart of Outlawell, feeding everyone who came by, bringing them in to the kitchen with the horsehair sofa and the Rayburn, providing soup at harvest time, the kettle always on. It was she who insisted on selling her house in Elgin to pay for a car for James (an insight into the value of houses and the cost of cars). And it was Jean who made James realise that he needed help on the farm, so introducing to the Outlawell story one of the most important figures in her grandson's life.

●

At the mart, men wanting work would stand and wait to be hired, and Geordie Gourlay was among them that day. He'd been brought up in the Aberlour orphanage, which had given him only a basic education and left him not knowing where or even when he'd been born. His feet weren't quite right, but when James asked around, it was Geordie that was recommended for his unshakeable honesty. He went with James to help at Outlawell, living in a bothy by the kitchen. Without Geordie, I get the impression that life on the farm would have been too much for James, who didn't keep well, and much lonelier for Hamish, who's surprising himself now by how emotional he's getting, talking about Geordie.

Sugar was Hamish's imaginary friend, who lived at the junction of the two roads out of the farm, but Geordie was his mentor. They'd hoe the fields of neeps together, and he shows me a photo of the two of them by the Fergie tractor, registration BSO 131. On my way in, I'd noticed a Fergie, slightly out of place parked to the side of the house in a cul-de-sac, with a very similar registration. Hamish hadn't managed to get the same one, but it's close enough.

When the family left the farm and his mother worked as a cook and housekeeper, she only took jobs that would offer a place for Geordie to live as well. She worked for Lord

Leven at Glenferness and the Morays at Darnaway, where Geordie had a flat over the stables below the castle. He stayed with the family right through to his death in 1994.

•

James Anderson, who'd taken Geordie on, had died long before him, in 1946. He'd wept only once in his life, as far as anyone could recall, at the funeral of his son James (Hamish) Falconer Anderson, another name from the Logie School register, who's buried at Edinkillie and remembered on the war memorial there. He was killed in 1942 at the age of 20 when his bomber crashed on a training mission in Somerset. He'd previously worked in the offices at Kinloss and been smarter – it was generally accepted – than his brothers John and Alastair. His nephew shows me a photo and hunts for more. 'He didn't suit war, and then he became a pilot, for goodness' sake,' says Hamish.

James, who had come home so damaged from the first war, had now lost his son to the second and was heard to vow that he would never volunteer for war again. He nonetheless found the heart to continue playing a part. Anyone standing and looking across the main road from Outlawell is seeing The Circle, a large area – now totally overgrown – which James cleared in order to grow crops for the war effort at home. He stabled his horse down there by Ramphlat Toll and dug for victory, gouging out roots, hauling timber and slashing at undergrowth. By the time he'd finished, the war was more or less over.

In later life his widow, Hamish's granny Jean, loved to walk round cemeteries. It's a funny thing, says Hamish, but now he likes to do it too. 'There are a lot from school now: there's something nice and something sad about it,' and it strikes me that his stories have been exactly like that. Sad ones, to be sure, but something nice in the telling of them, in the saving of these histories from the second sadness of forgetting.

No: 1656, John Ross, Logie Home Farm.

1962

'I never saw a starry sky again.'

Logie Home Farm • John Roderick Ross

John Ross is a great talker, but there's someone else I wish I could meet too.

His mother Jean first appears in John's story, by implication, on an autumn morning in 1957. He was born in the back bedroom in the house behind us: No. 2, at what is now Logie Steading. It was half past five in the morning and his dad came in from seeing to the cattle. 'You've got a son,' said the midwife. She was married to the auctioneer so I guess she'd have understood a farmer's priorities at that time of the day. 'My dad came through,' says John. 'He took a look. And then went back for his breakfast.'

The way he tells it, I almost believe John remembers the day, his father Sandy glancing into the crib, his mother getting up to wash the sheets of the bed he'd been born in. These stories handed down, these images of Logie Home Farm: 'He had a tractor with no cab, just a beret on his head, happy as a lord out there, ploughing these fields.'

The thing about John's storytelling is that it brings to life the sounds of his childhood: the splash of the bull pool in the Findhorn, where the Jerseys and Ayrshires go to drink and the children learn to swim, the calls of the Grant boys echoing in the woods as they come down from Braehead, the chimes of the clock in the yard by which his father sets his pocket watch, the purr of his Grandad Fraser's Jag and the rush of the wind as the children ride on the running board. Maybe that sense is amplified by the feeling of enclosure in the farmyard where we're standing, now the Logie Steading courtyard but then the centre of the family's life.

His dad might have been the tractorman but his mother was clearly the driving force, with five children and a job in the big house too, keeping three hundred hens, putting the eggs in wooden boxes and onto the bus and away, baking and cleaning and cooking and altering each child's clothes to pass down the line to the next. She'd think nothing of cycling to Burghead to see her brother, although the family did once have a car, for a day. She hadn't liked it so it hadn't stayed. The house was extended to keep pace with the family, but still the three boys shared a bed, across the room from their parents.

We are at the end of the yard, an art gallery to our left, a café opposite and his childhood home behind us to the right, and John talks me round the Home Farm as it was: the iron gates long gone but their bases still visible in the cobbles at our feet, the dairy beyond the bookshop, the silage pit where the café is, the cattle troughs now used as planters. I notice he's speaking as if the past is now: 'My dad's coming out here with a dung spreader, with my little sister on his knee and his little tractor.' And, turning round, 'Have they straightened it? No, it's there, see?' The bend in the railings where his brother Sandy got his head stuck and had to be jemmied out.

All five Rosses went up the hill to Logie School: Betty, Cathy, Sandy, John and David. 'You wanted to go to school, you couldn't wait,' says John. Except, I suppose, the children whose collars were grubby, whose necks were scrubbed raw with carbolic in front of the rest of the class. Or those who hated semolina and found themselves forced to eat it. You'd never say if you got a beating, as you'd only get another one at home. 'Everyone survived it,' says John, an odd phrase for what he says was the best time of his life. But everyone was equal, or at least that's how it felt, and no one had a better dress sense than anyone else. Each week, everyone from school would see each other again at Sunday school: John loved the Bible he'd got for his christening, and read it front to back. He loved the singing, too, and told his mother he'd be a minister (although the fact that the minister had a car might have played a part in that).

And then, when John was seven, Logie Home Farm was no longer his home. A new manager brought change. His father, the tractorman, was asked to milk cows and wasn't happy with that, so he moved the family to the Hays at Moss-side, and then to a new job in Forres.

Until then, the children had taken turns to go to town on a Saturday, a five-weekly rota of being marched to Granny Ross at Bogton Road while their mother did the shopping. And as John speaks, it's as if we're there on Tolbooth Street and can see the driver through the window of the Red Lion, draining his pint and his dram as the last of the shopping is loaded into the side of the bus, then heading up to take the wheel for home.

It was a shock for John and David to be pulled from Logie and landed at Applegrove, fish out of water in a town which had until then played a small part in their life. 'They were all strangers. They were townies. We wore shorts. No one wore shorts. We never had streetlights. The moon and the stars, they were our streetlights. I never saw a starry sky again.' His life now revolved round Boys Brigade and football, Sunday school a thing of the past. And everything was changing: John was one of the first intake to the new Forres Academy, as well as in the first year that had to wait to turn 16 before they could leave.

The people he'd known, though, stayed with him: Mrs Reid at the Post Office, her husband Bill the joiner; the estate workers off on their annual trip to Grantown; the girl who drowned at Relugas. We talk about the stories John will pass on: about how he got every job by word of mouth and juggled work with bringing up two children, and his second wedding, booked hastily for the day before covid locked the world down, when no one knew what life would soon be like.

As we say goodbye, I think of the bend in the railings, unnoticed by everyone here but John yet taking him straight back to the day it happened. And I think how none of us know when we wake in the morning if a wonky bit of railing of our own will come along, some detail which will find its way into our own particular stories, to be forever handed down as family history.

No: 1668, Marianne Nicolson, Regaul.

'With love, security and good teachers, you can't go too far wrong..'

Regaul • Marianne Nicolson

It hadn't really struck me until I spoke to Marianne Nicolson that, even in the era when she was at school, coming from Dunphail might define what people thought you could achieve. I wasn't surprised that girls were not expected do certain things: when the factor heard from her father Donald that she was going to be a doctor, he tried to put him straight: 'Oh, but a nurse, surely?' There was also the assumption that boys would go onto the farm, so everyone – girls and boys – got their (un)fair share of expectation from the world around them. But the reaction of a farmer friend near Brodie – 'Fancy that, going to university from a wee placie like that!' – tells a story about the area in which Marianne, her sister Lynn and brothers Grant and Davie grew up.

Marianne's story pins her career choice onto a single day, before she was old enough to be at school. 'Mother was going off to the church one day and, you know, with four kids and a farmer husband, where lunch is to be on the table at twelve o'clock come hell or high water, she was running late. And as she rushed out, she squished my finger in the door and had to take me to Leanchoil to have the nail removed. And the smell of the hospital, the atmosphere, I just loved it all.' As a treat, Marianne was taken by Margaret to choose a toy at Alec Stuart's shop and she chose a doctor's set, carefully placing it on the piano at home, out of the reach of her brother Grant. 'And then, of course, when people ask you what you want to do and you say you want to be a doctor, they're impressed, so I thought, 'Well, I'd better find out what that means, then!'

Except I wonder if all families would have encouraged the idea? Would some have told a girl of that age not to be so silly, that there'd be time to talk about that later? And not all schools, of course, had a Jean Maciver, a teacher who became a family friend and for whom, says Marianne, the Nicolson girls were as close to family as she ever got apart from her husband John, himself a fiercely clever man.

Jean was a highly dramatic woman, from what Marianne says, very aware of her public persona and able to inspire Marianne to strive to impress her. Even after a long and successful career in medicine, becoming professor of oncology at Aberdeen, Marianne still shudders at the memory of forgetting the word igloo and so failing to please her new teacher at their very first meeting. The schooling at Logie, says Marianne, was second to none, with English in the morning and maths in the afternoon; it was rare to have a day outside because classroom learning was just too important. The older children would support the younger ones, Marianne helping Alan Dawson with his reading. In the school room, still in the old building at that time, the children were placed so that Jean, the perfectionist, could see them all from where she presided at her desk. The register shows how numbers climbed dramatically when Dunphail School, the only other school in the immediate area, closed in 1966.

Just as Marianne's dream of being a doctor was imbued with the hospital smell of Leanchoil, it's the remarkably musty dampness of wellies and coats in the school porch, the freshness of Jean's Gold Spot breath spray and the scent of her Nulon hand cream, which she always applied as she came into class, which stay with Marianne and her sister Lynn. 'She was fabulous in every way,' says Marianne, her teacher a slim and beautiful woman with fantastic posture who had gone at 16 to study languages at Manchester University and then went on to study drama, but who felt overshadowed by her brother who had chosen medicine. The more Marianne talks, the more extraordinary Jean sounds, from her distressed crying at christenings (she had cats which she adored, but no children) to her dignified bearing at her husband's funeral: head back, voice strong, in full performance mode. 'It was her public and that is what she had to do.'

Performance was key at Logie, too. For drama productions, the children were drilled and schooled until they were word-perfect, giving them a confidence in public speaking which would stay with them a lifetime, as would the words of French which Jean taught them. They were entered into the Moray Music Festival, and toured *The Stolen Prince* when Marianne was just five, Lynn's character married to Mike Reid and the lead played by Geordie Paton. Marianne remembers Jean's quiet, seething fury when Graham 'Ping' Macgillivray made a minor slip in his words at Glenerney Little Theatre. 'Her standards were very, very high.'

Marianne loved school and worked hard, but then she worked hard on the farm as well, as was expected. There was no room for pretension in the family so anyone with airs and graces, thinking that they were the clever one, would be shot down in a moment. Life was straightforward. 'To Mother and Dad's great credit, we are as tight now as we were when we were little. And all four of us are very strong characters. Our table was the most thumped table anywhere.'

There are very many Nicolsons in the Logie register from the various branches of the family, and many more have been there – including Chloe now – since the entries stopped in 1979. A strong female line, says Marianne, began with her grandmother Elsie Coutts, born in 1890, who had been to college in Aberdeen. Living on the family farm in the hills at Feakirk, she'd cycle the ten miles or so to work in Forres: the family has a photo of her posing with one of the enormous typewriters of her day. Looking around for a husband, she saw that John Nicolson was a good cattle dealer, married him and had seven children. John died when Marianne's father Donald was just four, so Elsie took advice on how to keep the farm going, went into dairy and eventually passed the mantle on to her eldest son Stuart, Marianne's uncle.

Regaul, the tenant farm where Marianne grew up, was not a good farm, the land so wet that a lot of time went on unsticking tractors. Donald did think about buying somewhere but he didn't like debt, so began instead to diversify into contracting, bringing

Grant and Davie into the business. The family moved in 1975 from Regaul to Feakirk and Donald suffered his first heart attack on the day Davie, the youngest, left school, meaning for him that the door to agricultural college had closed.

Marianne moved on, taking a gap year before it was the fashion. She wanted to go to Canada with Grant, but he had skills that Canada wanted while she did not, so she spent half of the year as an auxiliary nurse and the other half working with the Dunphail gamekeepers before heading to study in Edinburgh. Her sister had gone to Aberdeen University and she really wanted to be different, but 'Dunphail was always key and core.' She'd come home to play in the dance band and her mother always set up a job for her in the summer, to be sure she would return. Ramages the fruit shop was fun, mostly because she got to do deliveries in a BMW 3.2 injection, flying over to Inverness and dawdling back to use up the time. 'And I'd decided at 11 that I'd marry Robbie Fraser, so he didn't stand a chance.'

The church, with Mr Duff the minister – a moral philosopher as well as a churchman, who'd throw out ethical questions to the congregation based on whatever was in the news that week – the youth club, the village hall badminton, the Scouts and Young Farmers (for the boys, that is) all offered a foundation for the Nicolsons which Marianne credits with their various successes. They felt loved, secure and were encouraged, with good teachers and mentors, and they didn't go too far wrong.

No: 1686, Andy Watt, Gardeners Cottages.

‘You did as you were told and you didn’t have opinions..’

Gardeners Cottages • Andrew Watt

On the day I meet Andy Watt, I’m running late, and I find him sitting waiting for me in his car in the Logie school playground. He’s had a lot to catch up on in those few minutes, though: it’s fifty-five years since he was last here.

So why has he never been back? ‘I’ve had no reason to. Life moves on.’

Which would have made me wonder if Logie was important to him after all, had he not been one of the first to come forward with his story. It can’t have been because of the school itself, although we take a look around. We run through the obvious differences between the place he knew and the school as it is now, the physical changes that are plain to see: his classrooms were in the old building which is now the school hall; the toilets used to be outside in the yard; the road which ran past the school is today the lay-by; the play area is now larger and neater; the shop by the gate has gone. We’re soon done with all that, though, and we’re on to the people.

Logie was the last of Andy’s three primary schools: he was at Rafford till it closed in 1963, Forres Primary – now called Applegrove – and finally, for two years, Logie, which was his favourite. Andy’s life then was spent within two close communities: the estate at Altyre and the school. He lived on Altyre because his mother was the cook in the big house. For nearly two years, Doreen Syzling had made the journey to work and back again on foot from their home in Newtyle Forest to the south. The house was more than three miles from the nearest tarred road and didn’t get electricity until 1962, when Andy was seven. After those years of walking, his mother was offered No 2, Gardeners Cottages (or The Gardens, as the register has it) on Altyre, making work – and life – that much easier.

There were big squads working on Altyre then, says Andy: twenty or so in forestry and another ten working on the farm and in the new dairy, built in the mid-1960s on the site of the old Altyre House. The shooting side had four keepers, two hill keepers and a kennel boy. ‘It was beautiful,’ he says, the drive always neatly edged and the grass well kept, curling matches on the ice in winter, and no one who didn't belong there ever walking through.

For the children, there was no question of not earning money as soon as you could and no question, when you had, that you handed some of it to your parents. The estate had jobs that children could do: the shoots needed beaters and for children they paid well, given that they would normally have no money at all. The nursery provided scythes for tidying round the trees, while there were also tatties to be picked at Sandy Simpson's at Longley. It's not as if everyone on there was happy, though: it was hard work, wages were low and money was always short. Living in tied houses meant accepting how things were.

Andy would occasionally cycle to Forres with friends, but he'd been called a country bumpkin when he moved from Rafford to Forres Primary and he didn't want too much to do with the town. The train line from Forres – until it closed in 1965 – had passed only half a mile from the door of their house in the forest, though, and in the era of steam two engines were needed for the long pull up the hill to Dunphail. They would burn a lot of coal and spew out sparks to either side, especially in icy weather when the wheels spun. Andrew, Andy's dad, worked with the Forestry Commission and would go on fire watch by the house: strapping a massive radio onto his back, he would set off onto the embankment ready to beat out any small blazes himself and calling for help on the radio if the fire became too fierce for him to handle on his own. Andy would take him his piece and people would wonder why his dad couldn't just carry his own: they didn't know how heavy that radio was.

The bus – itself a mini community of its own – took Andy to school every day. It was a disappointment when the old Calders bus conked out at Craigroy one day, just after they'd dropped the Macgillivrays home. Joe Fraser, who'd only recently taken over the business from Geordie Calder, invested in a new one – in the end, he'd have a fleet of ten – but this was a backward step as far as the children were concerned. It had seats you weren't allowed to kick and floors that had to be kept clean. Joe didn't like them getting up from their seats too early, and Andy remembers the lot of them flung to the floor when he slammed on the brakes to teach them a lesson.

His happiest memories are of school picnics at Hopeman; calling in on the Reids for sweets from the shop by the school gate, once it had moved from its original spot on the Pitteneask brae, at the end of what's now the driveway to Logie Steading; a school production of *The Mikado* which toured the district, the costumes hand-made by Mrs Maciver, with Andy playing the executioner and performances at Miss Bruce's at Glenerney, at Nairn and in the Town Hall in Forres; his first cigarette, after Scouts in the field below the school.

As for the classroom, he liked the Macivers well enough and accepted the strap as part of life. Wednesdays were Andy's worst day of the week, with a trip to the seawater pool at Nairn and just salad and soup with no pudding for lunch. I'm hoping for his sake that it was a Wednesday morning when he became a hero for the day, throwing up on the headmaster and forcing the school to close early while Mr Maciver went home to change.

The headmaster and his wife gave the six leavers a party in their house on the day they went off to Forres Academy, not guessing, I suppose, that a simple invitation to their house would form a lifelong memory. And it's easy to see, after all, why Andy has never felt the need to come back up the hill from Forres to Logie School: the communities he belonged to are still in his head, wherever he is when he's telling their stories.

No: 1846, Paul Coutts, Knockyfin.

'Things change..'

Knockyfin • Paul Coutts

The Coutts family had a fair few people knocking on the door to ask if they knew where the Lost Valley might be before it struck them that they might be living in it. They still don't know where the reference comes from, but when Paul was growing up, beyond the viaduct did feel like a very separate kind of place, invisible from the main road, served only by bumpy tracks, with few vehicles passing the door. Winters could see the Coutts snowed in for a week at a time, the fences buried deep.

Paul's great-grandfather had started life as a shepherd way up at remote Shenvault, well beyond Feakirk, and was offered the tenancy of Dallasbraughty by Altyre Estate in 1934, starting the Coutts family's connection with farming in Dunphail. And the story Paul tells me from when he was five, visiting the Dunphail smiddy where horseshoes were forged on the fire, working the bellows for Beal McTavish whose brother John – another Logie School pupil – had died in the First World War, makes me expect some emotional attachment to the land. But that's not what I get at all.

'I'm not really the normal farmer. A lot of farmers, all they think about is farming. I've never been like that. I think, why? What's the point in farming if that's all you can do and there's no time for anything else?' So farming is a job, just like any other: a way to make a living, not a way of life.

Paul had grown up knowing that there wasn't enough work on the farm to justify his coming home to it, so was planning on being an engineer. Just as he was going into his fifth year at Forres Academy, though, his dad Jim and his uncle Alan were offered the chance by Altyre to double the amount of land they farmed, taking on Tomnamoon, Johnstripe and Wester Greens. It was an offer they could only accept if Paul worked with them, so that's what he did. Now, though, Paul's two children have plans of their own so when he retires (and he says it won't be as late as his dad did) he'll be handing back the tenancy.

And that's just how it is, he says: things change. And as a child who went to Logie School in the mid-1970s, the stories he tells me look both ways: back in time to the black-smith with memories of the First World War and forward to the time when farming will be like any other job, a way of earning a living with no obligation on your children to do it too.

•

When he was at Logie School – his first headmaster Bill Young, and Margaret Camp-bell in the kitchen – it was still very much for local children. 'Nobody came into the school from outside. Back at that time, you weren't aware of more than just here. Now they know about the whole world, but back then, we didn't have all that.' I wondered, then, what it was like to work with his dad and uncle, thinking it all might be a little too close for comfort for a teenager. But then I hadn't reckoned on the water skiing.

In one extraordinary period in the 1980s, three of the Scottish national water ski team lived above the viaduct in Edinkillie: Jim Coutts, his son Paul and Ewan Hunter. Paul was just fourteen when he represented Scotland for the first time.

'Because we skied together, and we played badminton in the hall as well, it was easier, we had things outside work to do together. We worked long days during the week to be able to ski together at the weekends. That was our thing, and we made time for it.'

•

For Paul, one of the great things about this place used to be that everyone was known. If someone was new, you'd know all about them before they knew you.

I remembered a story of my own from my first days in Edinkillie. Newly arrived from Birmingham and living in a house behind the church, I thought I should go and introduce myself one Sunday. There turned out to be no need. 'We know who you are,' said one church elder. In fact, come to think of it, that might well have been Jim Coutts.

'I don't know half the people here now,' says his son Paul. 'People come in and are gone in a year. That never happened. There are a lot more people going past the house, but they're not people you know.' Whist drives at the hall were a serious business, Nellie Simpson of Balvlair, fur stole round her shoulders, barking at the children if they put the wrong card down. There was badminton and bowls and ceilidhs, everyone knowing who'd be there. They'd go to each other's houses on a Saturday night, play cards and talk.

So yes, as Paul said at the start, things change. A lot of his schoolfriends left for university and never came back so the change is not confined to farming. And maybe, now I think about it, that's part of the appeal of the school register: its reassuring, repeating pattern giving a sense of solid continuity, even though we know that things can change in the turning of a page.

No: 1893, Fiona Swanson, Old Station House.

*'It became part of my childhood: you moved into
a house and decided which walls to knock down..'*

Old Station House • Fiona C. M. Swanson

Fiona Swanson doesn't so much tell a story as inhabit it. With just a few gestures, she's already summoned up her Guide leader Miss Murray, gripping the steering wheel of her brown Mini estate (and barely seeing over it) as she drove down the back road from where she lived at Windyridge. A few minutes before, Fiona had been a child again, peeping with her brother round their neighbour's kitchen door in the hope of a scoop of ice cream in blackcurrant and some Highlander shortbread, or maybe a piece of the best tablet in the world. And now she's flourishing an imaginary cake slice, as her mother always did with a real one, reminding the family of the many long hours she spent pointing the stonework of the Old Station House when it was halfway to being a home.

In the mid-1970s Fiona's parents Ron and Sue Swanson had bought from Dunphail Estate the shell of the railway station which had closed in 1965. They lived in Broom of Moy and travelled up to Dunphail to work on making the station a habitable home. It was full of the paraphernalia of its former life, the sunken line of the track running alongside the house and a garden that was a perpetual treasure hunt, turning up mementos of the station as it once had been. The Swanson children thought it normal to have a railway platform in the garden and to find cattle branding irons in the bushes. And as part of the renovations, they knocked two downstairs rooms into one, setting the scene for a day which must have firmly established the former station as the Swanson family home.

The woman with the Highlander shortbread was Ann Munro who lived at The Laurels, at the other end of the station sidings. Born Ann Smith, she had trained as a nanny, then joined the Land Army and at some point acquired the nickname Smithy which stuck, even within her family. She had married a farmer, Beal Munro, and lived up beyond the viaduct at Lurg near the Beachens. Until, that is, the day when the chimney caught fire and Smithy threw a bucket of what she took to be water onto the hearth.

It was, in fact, paraffin and the farm burned right to the ground. What did 'the most philosophical woman in the world' do next? She simply moved to the Laurels and started again.

Ron's parents moved from Burghead to the Beachens to be near their family, and the time came when Fiona's grandmother needed care. Together, Fiona's mother and Smithy nursed her until her death in 1979. And about a year later, Fiona acquired what she calls a fifth grandparent when Smithy married Fiona's grandfather. The wedding ceremony was held at one end of the enormous living room of the Old Station House, the reception at the other, in what had been the ticket office and waiting room.

Fiona had a very mobile childhood, moving from one school and even from one country to another; her name had first caught my eye in the register, in fact, as having left Logie for Saudi Arabia, an exotic Cause of Leaving even for the late 1970s. That was a short-lived stay, though, as her father's job as a port administrator was soon reconfigured to being of 'Bachelor Status', meaning that his family was not permitted to remain. Fiona came back as a boarder in Moffat, two hundred miles or so away, adding another school to an already long list – she'd been to four by the time she was seven – but the Old Station House remained the family home until 1982.

Working on the principle that it's only the extremes of emotion that we recall, Fiona's brief time at Logie Primary must have been happy, she says, because she can't remember all that much about it. In fact, so connected is she with the school that her own memories and those from later, from the time of her daughter and her niece, are hard for her to distinguish. Maybe that says something about how little had changed in between. Her own days there came to an end when her mother got a job at Moray College in Elgin, meaning that it made more sense for her to drop Fiona at Applegrove School on the way.

As a child so used to moving on, Fiona remembers Dunphail as a welcoming place to live. The church – with 'the legendary' Mrs McColl-Poole as minister – was important to the family, sitting in the same pew week by week, her mother running the Sunday school in Edinkillie hall after the service. The visit of the van from Stables, the grocer in Forres, was a highlight, the newspaper delivered on Sundays with chocolate as a bonus, but gradually, with the family growing up, there were more and more trips in the blue-and-white camper van down to Forres and back. Winters were hard, the Swansons having to dig their way out every time the snow plough cleared the road and dumped the snow on their track in passing. It began to be too much: it was time to move on. After all their efforts at the Old Station House, Fiona's parents did what they always did and took on another house to do up. They stayed in the area but started all over again.

However much sense it made, it was very hard for her mother to leave the Old Station House. 'She absolutely loved it,' says Fiona. It was years before Sue was able even to drive past, always choosing to take the Ferness road if the family went south.

Fiona says this life of movement has made her resilient, if what she calls childlike, compensating for having had to grow up before she was ready to. She came back to live in the area, just a few miles closer to Forres, on Valentine's Day 2002. And if it was continuity she was seeking, then she found it: she was delighted to find the same postie delivering mail, the one she'd known as a child at the Old Station House.

No: 1910, Scott Taylor, South Lodge.

'It didn't feel different, it was just what was normal..'

South Lodge • Scott Taylor

There's a certain symmetry to the Admission Register: look at the very first and the very last pages and you'll find the child of a Logie Estate gamekeeper. Cath Macdonald, the daughter of William, joined Logie School in 1883, a few days short of her sixth birthday, followed by her brothers Alexander and Donald and little sister Maggie. Nearly a century later, the children of Davie Taylor, a keeper on Logie Estate since 1969, were also to join Logie School: David was followed by his brother Scott and their sister Ann, who came to the school after the register had fallen out of use.

Their father had started work at Logie in the days of a whole team of keepers, as there would have been in William Macdonald's day. The register doesn't say where the Macdonalds lived – it must just have been obvious to whoever was making the entry. They might even have come to school from South Lodge as David, Scott and Ann Taylor did, but wherever it was, William's house would have been at one of the gates: keeping people out was part of a keeper's job. There'd have been plenty to poach back then: salmon, grouse, hares, rabbits, although fewer deer than today, and – another big difference between now and then, says Davie – the keeper's word was law.

William Macdonald is listed as a rabbit trapper on the birth certificates of the older children, but when their sister Maggie was born in 1884, the registrar granted him the title of gamekeeper, as the Logie School register had from the start. That first page of the register is a fascinating insight into how people locally earned their living, often listing the jobs that the pupils' fathers did: running down the page, you'll find a blacksmith at Altyre; a mason at Sluie; a grieve at Altyre; a farmer at Presley; a shepherd at Longlea; a cattleman at Blairs and – against three families on just this opening page – 'S Fisher, Sluie', testifying to the numbers of salmon in the river then.

•

The fact that Logie School was only a short walk across the field from South Lodge meant that Scott, David and Ann Taylor could always make it in, whatever the weather: in fact, very few school days must ever have been missed by anyone, given the number of parents with tractors and ploughs who could get the children in for class, however deep the snow. At this stage, the register shows that the school was still serving the same local patch that it always had. Having only a few yards between home and school also meant that the boys' mother Glenis could watch from the back door as they hurtled down the banky, the run from school to the bottom pitch often made in half a canoe that their dad Davie had salvaged from the river; he'd padded the fence with square bales to make it safe, once someone had broken a bone in a crash on the bend.

Davie Taylor was to stay as keeper at Logie Estate until his retirement in 2012 and, as with most people who are asked about their childhood, his son Scott says that what his dad did made no real difference, that the life of a keeper's son was really just normal.

Although now you ask me, he says, not everyone went home to pheasants to pluck, ferrets to see to and sticks to cut. Most children would not have thought about the river-banks that needed mowing or the dogs that needed feeding. Most would not have gone beating for grouse at weekends or spent Christmas breaks on pheasant shoots. There wasn't anything to spend your money on in Dunphail so the cash soon added up. Not many, he supposes, learnt to deal with lords and sirs, to know how to address them, to mind their manners and speak only if spoken to. Life was always busy, as his parents' lives were, and when Glenis would go to Orkney to see family, the boys would spend days with their father, his work their day-to-day life.

Scott's brother David is a keeper himself now, while Scott is an estate farm manager. He's never had a day out of work since he left school in 1988, thanks largely, he says, to his start in life in Dunphail. 'It fairly helped when we left school. There wasn't an opportunity to walk to Forres and sit in the High Street and do nothing – we had to do something. There was always a job to do, always. It's just what we did.'

Heather Parker, Logie School.

'We got the local paper and we thought, 'Why not?''

Logie School • Heather Parker

With a snap of the fingers, Heather Parker shows me how quickly and decisively her life changed.

She's talking about 1977 when, on the spur of the moment, her husband Ron answered an advertisement for the job of foreman forester on Dunphail Estate. When he was offered it, Heather had two weeks to hand in her notice at work and move, with Ron and their two children, from Yorkshire to The Dorran on Dunphail, a tiny and very damp estate house, now demolished. She brought skills with her – she taught guitar and ran a pre-school playgroup – but only Ron had a job to come to. It was a big move in many ways, hundreds of miles from everything familiar. They swapped their family home for what Heather calls a tiny little doll's house, they moved from a community in which they had friends to one where they had none, from a place where her humour made people laugh to one where it didn't and from a society where they fitted to one where she felt like a total outsider.

Coming in to Dunphail, Heather viewed the relationship between landowners and tenants in the 1970s as that of master and servant. It was a struggle to find her place. 'Everybody knew everybody.' It's the first story in which I hear this as a negative, but then it's one of the few stories I've heard that's from someone who wasn't born here.

For his part, Ron was happy in his forester's job and her children were settled as pupils at Logie but it took five years or so for Heather to feel at home. Starting to work at the school was a huge part of that shift. She had set up a playgroup in the school hall and was then asked by the headteacher Ian Black (better known elsewhere as the former Olympic swimmer) to take up a teaching post, an invitation which turned into twenty-five years of working with a succession of headteachers: next came Ruth Bowman, Ian Brodie and Irene Ross.

Heather's time at Logie School began just as the Admission Register was about to fall out of use. The school was still completely rural, she says, when she began in 1978 but she gradually saw it change, with more people wanting to send their children up to Logie for what they considered its different ambience, its smaller class sizes and its outdoor environment. The school remained reliant on local families, though, and it felt the impact if they moved away. Heather still remembers the day when Mrs Grant came to break the news that the school was to lose her four children, as the family was moving from Altyre to the newly built council houses at Thornhill on the edge of Forres. Their house there, adds Heather, was always recognisable: where others had hedges and flowers, the Grants had pristine rows of tatties.

In the end, Heather and her family stayed in their tiny doll's house on Dunphail Estate for thirteen years. The couple then moved to the Beachens where Ron worked at his real passion, wood sculpture. After his death, their daughter worried about Heather, living there beyond the viaduct and – more to the point – beyond the more-than-steep climb of kirk brae, often impassable in winter, but there's no sense from Heather that even though she moved to Elgin, she ever really wanted to leave Dunphail. So what made her do it? The answer is simple: 'Old age!'

No: 1936, Steven Thain, Wester Greens.

‘When you look back, you just think of a playground, a million acres in size..’

Wester Greens • Steven Thain

Steven Thain can barely remember Logie School. His name's there in the register, the last but one, but his days were spent planning his next escape. Not because he had anything against Logie in particular, but because his whole life was a bid for freedom. Even at home, he'd hide under the hedge while his mother searched the house and garden and then the house again, Steven just waiting for his chance to get away.

He was very good at going missing. He'd hear the drone of the forager across the field from school at breaktime and be off, bolting into the trees and away. He'd will the snow to fall more heavily so that everyone could be sent home. He'd be coaxed by his sisters to sit still and listen in class, but all he wanted was to be on the farm. And, to its credit, Logie School seemed to understand his need for freedom, simply sending older children to track him down and bring him back, until the next time.

The school did offer him something, though, which he took for granted until he moved away. The pupils at Logie spoke a common language, one that he didn't find elsewhere. The children of farmers and cattlemen, tractormen and keepers, they were mini adults, he says, talking about things they'd heard about at home: harvesting, herding, ploughing and stalking.

His father Joe worked for Altyre Estate and Steven still can list the names of the men who worked with him: Eric James from Rafford; 'auld Sandy'; Michie, Geddes and the Allardes and Kenny Boag. 'It was brilliant.'

The part these men play in the story Steven tells me shows how his tight-knit community worked. As he talks, I think how distant in time it feels and am surprised to remember that we're nearly at the end of the register.

•

As Steven tells the story of the day he nearly died, I have to remind myself that he was only four. He says that he wasn't in pain at first: tractors were flying in and out of the yard, the drivers not noticing that the boy was lying trapped below a fallen gate just beside the silage pit. He'd been watching them work, balancing on the top bar until he crashed to the ground, his head just missing the concrete. His sisters long since gone to the house for their tea, he lay there for hours, or at least it felt that way, until at last he was spotted and carried inside. It was then, with the pressure off, that the pain really came but no one knew that he'd broken both his legs.

Of that evening, a very strong image remains in Steven's mind: ten, eleven, maybe twelve men gathered together in the house, come in from the farm when they'd heard the news. All had known Steven since the day he was born. They do not leave but wait and keep watch, telling the doctor – who when Steven's mother first calls him is unwilling to come out – that they'll be down to fetch him if he doesn't show his face.

That feeling of community, of being protected and supported by the people who've known you longest and know you best, seems to sum up Steven's feelings about his life in Dunphail. He had enormous freedom for a child but knew that he was safe, someone always watching for him from their house or picking him up and taking him home if it was getting dark. Within the bounds of a few miles, he was free, striking out across fields to where the tractors were working and coming home only to sleep or to eat. Everyone knew him and understood what he was like.

All that changed when he moved north with his family to Tain. Living just a mile from the town, Steven found that no one spoke the language of the countryside – or the school – that he'd left.

•

Steven's been driving around, looking at how the land is being kept, even though in the end he didn't stay in farming. He talks of how sorry he is that his children didn't have the childhood he had, and wonders if he might come back here. I ask how he feels about the changes in the community about him. Can he see any advantage to people moving in from outside, changing the place bit by bit? I don't even get to finish the question. 'No,' he replies. For him, the safety of his childhood came from knowing exactly who everybody was, and from them knowing him.

No: 1937, Zinnia Watt, Gardeners Cottages.

'We were just one big, happy family..'

Gardeners Cottages • Zinnia Jane Watt

Zinnia Watt is the last name in the Admission Register discovered in the office at Logie Primary. It tells us that she joined in an intake of nine children on 21 August 1979 and her memories of the place echo many of those from the decades before her: it felt very much like a country school, its network of families, still largely working in farming and forestry, giving the children a feeling of real security. She remembers what many others do: the outdoor space, the friendliness, and the shock of the move to Forres Academy, where people behaved very differently and even dressed very differently.

But the part of her story she mentions first, before any of that, is that her mother was not married when she had Zinnia. 'I was born out of wedlock,' she says, and the use of that old-fashioned phrase somehow underlines how out-of-date it was beginning to be as a concept. While illegitimacy was frowned upon by some, she says it was only an issue when people asked where her father was, and most people didn't. This status had no real impact on her life, either day-to-day or long-term, with Zinnia living on Altyre Estate with her mother, her uncle and her grandparents – 'Just like the Waltons!' – knowing who her father was but only meeting him when she was about ten. 'Cushioned' is how she describes her upbringing at Logie School and on Altyre Estate.

•

This shift in attitudes towards children born outside marriage completes an arc in the Logie School register's stories from Annie in the first to Zinnia in the last, one whose illegitimate status was noted at every stage of her life, the other for whom it was largely irrelevant. While these individual stories can only reflect glimpses of bigger changes in society, they do allow an insight into the evolution of the community around Logie School and I owe heartfelt thanks to all the storytellers for sharing their family tales.

I'd also like to thank Logie Primary for keeping the Admission Register, even when it was no longer in use, and the bookbinder Elizabeth Lumsden for restoring it beautifully. I'm grateful to ScotlandsPeople and the Heritage service of Moray Libraries for helping me research these stories; to Paul Heartfield for his photography and design, to Hannah Rodway for her work on mapping, to the Finderne Development Trust for their support with printing costs, to David Ritchie and Keith Whittles for their interest and advice and, of course, to everyone who has bought this book, helping to support the work of Logie Primary today.

The Admission Register of Logie School holds many more stories within its pages; even those told here are just fragments of their particular family histories. I hope this book will inspire you, wherever you live, to recall and share your own tales, ask your own questions, record your own memories and, above all, to remember and honour the people who shaped your community.

The register	In this era of digital record keeping, it was a joy to find the Admission Register at Logie Primary and to know that I was turning pages that had been turned by my predecessors for nearly a century. The spine of the book was fragile so, as I opened it, I expected to find brittle, discoloured or faded pages. Instead, the ledger paper (Imperial, 22 x 30 ins) used by McDougall & Co, Publishers, Stationers and Booksellers of St James Square, Edinburgh had survived intact and made sure the register had done its job, keeping the records legible to this day. Now rebound, the *New Admission Register of Logie Undenominational (*sic*) School, Arranged to Meet the Regulations of the Scotch Education Department* will be good for another hundred years.

Moira Dennis has lived in Dunphail with her husband Roy for sixteen years, having moved from Birmingham where she had worked for the BBC as a radio producer. Their daughter Phoebe was a pupil at Logie Primary for seven years and Moira took up the post of school administrator there in 2021.

Paul Heartfield is a professional photographer. He has run his photography business together with his wife Ali for the past 23 years. In 2020 they moved up from London to Findhorn. His daughter Scout is a pupil at Logie Primary. Whilst specialising in editorial portrait photography, Paul also collaborates on projects focussing on half-forgotten or lost narratives, touring internationally with exhibitions such as the X-Ray Audio Project.

https://www.paulheartfield.photography

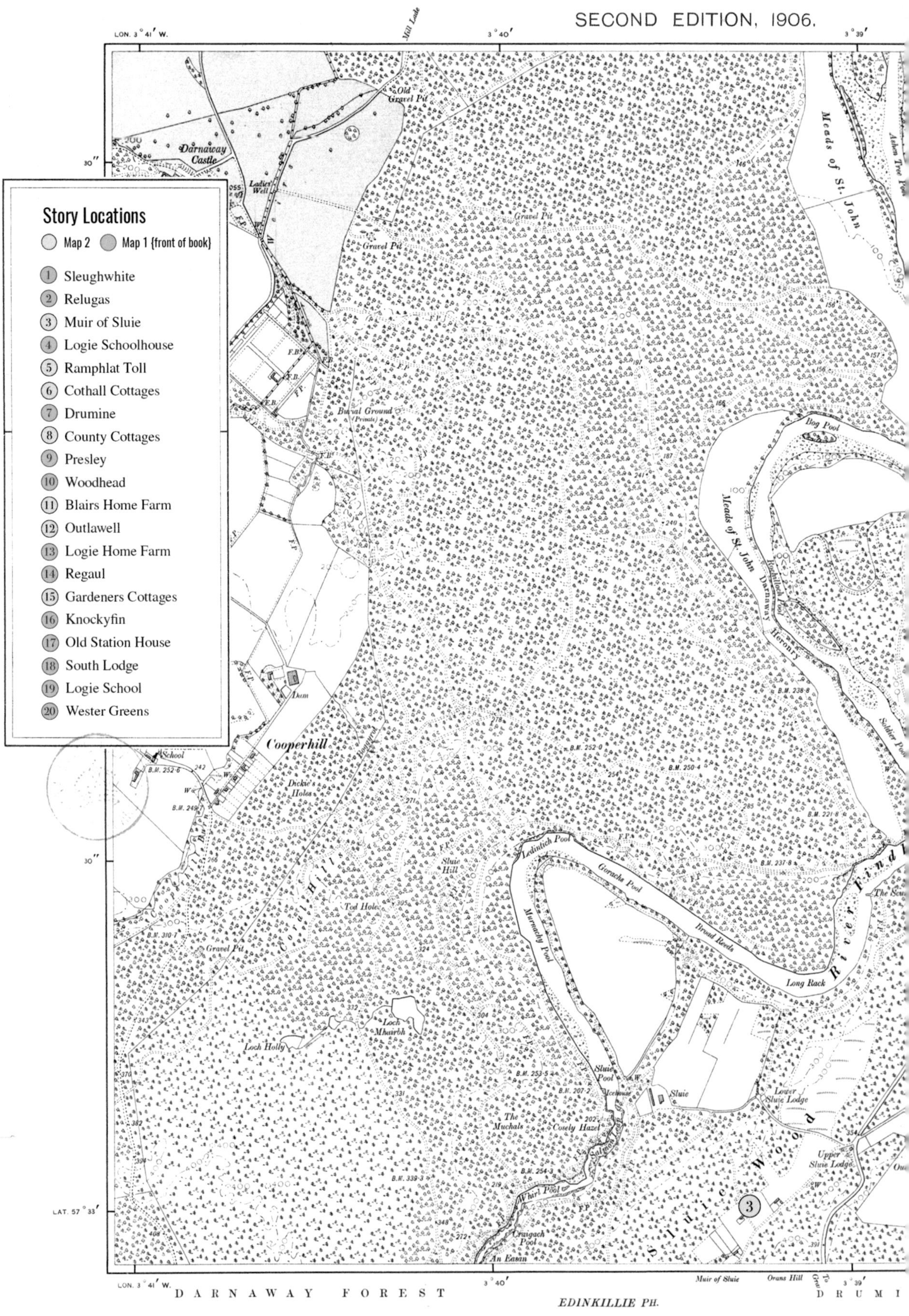

Story Locations

Map 2   Map 1 (front of book)

1. Sleughwhite
2. Relugas
3. Muir of Sluie
4. Logie Schoolhouse
5. Ramphlat Toll
6. Cothall Cottages
7. Drumine
8. County Cottages
9. Presley
10. Woodhead
11. Blairs Home Farm
12. Outlawell
13. Logie Home Farm
14. Regaul
15. Gardeners Cottages
16. Knockyfin
17. Old Station House
18. South Lodge
19. Logie School
20. Wester Greens

Darnaway Castle

Ladies' Well

Cooperhill

Burial Ground (Private)

Dickie's Holes

Sluie Hill

Tod Holes

Gravel Pit

Loch Mhairbh

Loch Holly

The Muchals

Cosey Hazel

An Easan

Craigach Pool

Whir' Pool

Sluie Pool

Meconnar

Sluie

Lower Sluie Lodge

Upper Sluie Lodge

Long Rack

Broad Reeds

Gorrachs Pool

Mermaddy Pool

Ardintich Pool

Dog Pool

Meads of St. John

Meads of St. John

Gravel Pit

Gravel Pit

Old Gravel Pit

Mill Leade

3

DARNAWAY FOREST

EDINKILLIE PH.

Muir of Sluie   Oruns Hill   DRUMI

River Findhorn

Sluie Wood